Physician-Assisted Suicide

POINT COUNTERPOINT

American Military Policy
Capital Punishment
Election Reform
Freedom of Speech
Gun Control
Legalizing Marijuana
The Limits of Search and Seizure
Mental Health Reform
Physician-Assisted Suicide
Religion in Public Schools
The Right to Privacy
Trial of Juveniles as Adults

Physician-Assisted Suicide

Alan Marzilli

SERIES CONSULTING EDITOR
Alan Marzilli, M.A., J.D.

CHELSEA HOUSE
P U B L I S H E R S
A Haights Cross Communications Company

Philadelphia

CHELSEA HOUSE PUBLISHERS

VP, NEW PRODUCT DEVELOPMENT   Sally Cheney
DIRECTOR OF PRODUCTION   Kim Shinners
CREATIVE MANAGER   Takeshi Takahashi
MANUFACTURING MANAGER   Diann Grasse

Staff for PHYSICIAN-ASSISTED SUICIDE

EDITOR   Patrick M.N. Stone
PRODUCTION ASSISTANT   Megan Emery
PHOTO EDITOR   Sarah Bloom
SERIES AND COVER DESIGNER   Keith Trego
LAYOUT   21st Century Publishing and Communications, Inc.

http://www.chelseahouse.com

First Printing

1 3 5 7 9 8 6 4 2

Library of Congress Cataloging-in-Publication Data

Marzilli, Alan.
   Physician-assisted suicide / by Alan Marzilli.
      p. cm.—(Point/counterpoint)
Includes index.
Contents: Death by prescription—People should have the right to determine
when and how they die—States should protect people from choosing suicide—
People should not have to make end-of-life decisions without medical advice—
Widespread legalization would have devastating effects on medical practice
and research—Modern medicine has increased the need for physician-assisted
suicide—Nothing justifies taking human lives—The future of physician-
assisted suicide.
   ISBN 0-7910-7485-4 (hc)
   1. Assisted suicide—Juvenile literature. [1. Assisted suicide.] I. Title. II. Series.
R726.M319 2003
179.7—dc21

                                                              2003009506

CONTENTS

Introduction
Alan Marzilli, M.A., J.D.
Durham, North Carolina

The debates presented in POINT/COUNTERPOINT are among the most interesting and controversial in contemporary American society, but studying them is more than an academic activity. They affect every citizen; they are the issues that today's leaders debate and tomorrow's will decide. The reader may one day play a central role in resolving them.

Why study both sides of the debate? It's possible that the reader will not yet have formed any opinion at all on the subject of this volume—but this is unlikely. It is more likely that the reader will already hold an opinion, probably a strong one, and very probably one formed without full exposure to the arguments of the other side. It is rare to hear an argument presented in a balanced way, and it is easy to form an opinion on too little information; these books will help to fill in the informational gaps that can never be avoided. More important, though, is the practical function of the series: Skillful argumentation requires a thorough knowledge of *both* sides—though there are seldom only two, and only by knowing what an opponent is likely to assert can one form an articulate response.

Perhaps more important is that listening to the other side sometimes helps one to see an opponent's arguments in a more human way. For example, Sister Helen Prejean, one of the nation's most visible opponents of capital punishment, has been deeply affected by her interactions with the families of murder victims. Seeing the families' grief and pain, she understands much better why people support the death penalty, and she is able to carry out her advocacy with a greater sensitivity to the needs and beliefs of those who do not agree with her. Her relativism, in turn, lends credibility to her work. Dismissing the other side of the argument as totally without merit can be too easy—it is far more useful to understand the nature of the controversy and the reasons *why* the issue defies resolution.

The most controversial issues of all are often those that center on a constitutional right. The Bill of Rights—the first ten amendments to the U.S. Constitution—spells out some of the most fundamental rights that distinguish the governmental system of the United States from those that allow fewer (or other) freedoms. But the sparsely worded document is open to interpretation, and clauses of only a few words are often at the heart of national debates. The Bill of Rights was meant to protect individual liberties; but the needs of some individuals clash with those of society as a whole, and when this happens someone has to decide where to draw the line. Thus the Constitution becomes a battleground between the rights of individuals to do as they please and the responsibility of the government to protect its citizens. The First Amendment's guarantee of "freedom of speech," for example, leads to a number of difficult questions. Some forms of expression, such as burning an American flag, lead to public outrage—but nevertheless are said to be protected by the First Amendment. Other types of expression that most people find objectionable, such as sexually explicit material involving children, are not protected because they are considered harmful. The question is not only where to draw the line, but how to do this without infringing on the personal liberties on which the United States was built.

The Bill of Rights raises many other questions about individual rights and the societal "good." Is a prayer before a high school football game an "establishment of religion" prohibited by the First Amendment? Does the Second Amendment's promise of "the right to bear arms" include concealed handguns? Is stopping and frisking someone standing on a corner known to be frequented by drug dealers a form of "unreasonable search and seizure" in violation of the Fourth Amendment? Although the nine-member U.S. Supreme Court has the ultimate authority in interpreting the Constitution, its answers do not always satisfy the public. When a group of nine people—sometimes by a five-to-four vote—makes a decision that affects the lives of hundreds of millions, public outcry can be expected. And the composition of the Court does change over time, so even a landmark decision is not guaranteed to stand forever. The limits of constitutional protection are always in flux.

These issues make headlines, divide courts, and decide elections. They are the questions most worthy of national debate, and this series aims to cover them as thoroughly as possible. Each volume sets out some of the key arguments surrounding a particular issue, even some views that most people consider extreme or radical—but presents a balanced perspective on the issue. Excerpts from the relevant laws and judicial opinions and references to central concepts, source material, and advocacy groups help the reader to explore the issues even further and to read "the letter of the law" just as the legislatures and the courts have established it.

It may seem that some debates—such as those over capital punishment and abortion, debates with a strong moral component—will never be resolved. But American history offers numerous examples of controversies that once seemed insurmountable but now are effectively settled, even if only on the surface. Abolitionists met with widespread resistance to their efforts to end slavery, and the controversy over that issue threatened to cleave the nation in two; but today public debate over the merits of slavery would be unthinkable, though racial inequalities still plague the nation. Similarly unthinkable at one time was suffrage for women and minorities, but this is now a matter of course. Distributing information about contraception once was a crime. Societies change, and attitudes change, and new questions of social justice are raised constantly while the old ones fade into irrelevancy.

Whatever the root of the controversy, the books in POINT/ COUNTERPOINT seek to explain to the reader the origins of the debate, the current state of the law, and the arguments on both sides. The goal of the series is to inform the reader about the issues facing not only American politicians, but all of the nation's citizens, and to encourage the reader to become more actively involved in resolving these debates, as a voter, a concerned citizen, a journalist, an activist, or an elected official. Democracy is based on education, and every voice counts—so every opinion must be an informed one.

For centuries, physicians have administered medications to hasten the slow death of the terminally ill patient. The practice attracted little attention until the 1990s, when Dr. Jack Kevorkian introduced his "suicide machine" and began to assist the suicides of dozens of people with terminal illness. The Supreme Court has ruled only that states *may* ban this practice; the states themselves must decide whether they *should*.

Civil libertarians, as well as people who want the right to end their lives as they choose, now fight for legalization—but they face strong opposition from doctors, religious and "right to life" groups, and many people with disabilities. Is there a constitutional right to control the human body? How far does it extend?

Death by Prescription

They call him "Doctor Death." Jack Kevorkian, a quirky, cantankerous Michigan physician, made headlines across the United States throughout the 1990s with an unwavering devotion to a very controversial cause: He helped people with chronic illnesses to end their suffering, not by curing them but by helping them to commit suicide.

Kevorkian, a pathologist who earned his nickname early in his career because of his fascination with death, decided after many years of professional ups and downs to make a career out of helping patients to die. He invented a "suicide machine" and even opened a "suicide clinic." Kevorkian's actions shocked the public because they represented the exact opposite of what many thought a physician's role should be—to help patients to *live*.

Kevorkian's actions also attracted the attention of the media, which publicized his involvement in the deaths of his

Dr. Jack Kevorkian, pictured here in 1991 with his "suicide machine," came to symbolize physician-assisted suicide in the 1990s. The key elements of his machine were its relatively painless chemicals and its trigger system; it enabled the patient to initiate his or her own death, which was meant to be like falling asleep. Kevorkian also used carbon monoxide poisoning and lethal injection. Legislators hurried to ban physician-assisted suicide, though, and in 1999, after the suicides of more than 100 patients, Kevorkian was convicted of second-degree murder in Michigan.

"patients," all of whom had expressed a desire to die. In 1990, he helped to end the life of Janet Adkins, a 54-year-old woman with Alzheimer's disease. He used his suicide machine, which injected first a sedative to put the person into a coma and then a second chemical that caused the heart to cease beating. The machine required the user to pull a trigger that initiated his or her own death. The following year, Kevorkian assisted the deaths of two women on the same day: Marjorie Wantz, who used the suicide machine, and Sherry Miller, who inhaled lethal carbon monoxide gas through a mask strapped to her face.

Although doctors have long responded to the pleas of suffer-ing patients by prescribing painkillers that could have the "double effect" of hastening the patient's death, Kevorkian's actions were markedly different. Not only did he devise procedures that were designed for the sole purpose of hastening death, but the defiant Kevorkian also publicized his actions and challenged the legal system to stop him from helping people commit suicide.

> • **Does the legal system have a special responsibility to punish people who openly defy the law?**

Kevorkian and the Courts

Legally speaking, what Kevorkian was doing was called physician-assisted suicide, meaning that the seriously ill person ends his or her own life, but does so with the help of a physician. Kevorkian had invented the suicide machine, supplied the lethal medications, and saw to it that the needle was inserted into the vein, but the patient pulled the trigger. With the carbon monoxide poisoning, the patient pulled a clothespin off the tube leading to a mask that was strapped over the mouth.

Many people commit suicide alone, which raises the question as to why a physician's help would be necessary. Supporters of physician-assisted suicide have claimed that the practice is necessary to help people whose ailments would impair their own ability to commit suicide, and that the involvement of the physician makes the suicide less traumatic for the person and the person's family.

Many condemned Kevorkian's actions, but it was not clear how Michigan law would respond. Although prosecutors tried to put Kevorkian behind bars, they were consistently foiled in their efforts. A judge dismissed murder charges in Adkins's death. After a series of legal maneuvers, a jury eventually acquitted Kevorkian of charges in the deaths of Wantz and Miller in 1996.

> • **Was Dr. Kevorkian assisting suicide or committing murder?**

In the meantime, "Doctor Death" continued his activities. He assisted in the deaths of other patients, despite the revocation of his medical license and the passage of a law banning physician-assisted suicide. Kevorkian remained defiant, even wearing outrageous costumes to court. Still, juries continued to acquit him, and Michigan's early attempts at banning physician-assisted suicide were declared unconstitutional. Around the country, terminally ill patients and their doctors raised similar challenges to other states' laws.

The Supreme Court Weighs In

In 1997, the U.S. Supreme Court turned its attention to physician-assisted suicide. The Court reviewed two cases in which federal appeals courts had declared that bans on the practice were unconstitutional: One court had ruled that a Washington law violated the Fourteenth Amendment's guarantee of "due process of law" and the other that a New York law violated the same amendment's guarantee of "equal protection of the laws." The

THE LETTER OF THE LAW

Michigan's Law on Murder

First-degree murder; penalty; definitions.
(1) A person who commits any of the following is guilty of first-degree murder and shall be punished by imprisonment for life:
  (a) Murder perpetrated by means of poison, lying in wait, or any other willful, deliberate, and premeditated killing.
  (b) Murder committed in the perpetration of, or attempt to perpetrate, arson, criminal sexual conduct in the first, second, or third degree, child abuse in the first degree, a major controlled substance offense, robbery, carjacking, breaking and entering of a dwelling, home invasion in the first or second degree, larceny of any kind, extortion, or kidnapping.
  (c) A murder of a peace officer or a corrections officer....

Second-degree murder; penalty.
All other kinds of murder shall be murder of the second degree, and shall be punished by imprisonment in the state prison for life, or any term of years, in the discretion of the court trying the same.

Source: Mich. Comp. Laws §§750.136–750.137

states had appealed the lower courts' rulings in an effort to keep physician-assisted suicide illegal in their states.

Reversing both appeals courts in decisions announced on the same day, the Supreme Court held in *Washington* v. *Glucksberg* that the bans on assisted suicide did not violate the due process clause:

> The history of the law's treatment of assisted suicide in this country has been and continues to be one of the rejections of nearly all efforts to permit it. That being the case, our decisions lead us to conclude that the asserted "right" to assistance in committing suicide is not a fundamental liberty interest protected by the Due Process Clause.[1]

• **Did the Framers of the Constitution ever consider whether assisted suicide should be legal?**

Similarly, in *Vacco* v. *Quill*, the Court ruled that, although the equal protection clause "embodies a general rule that States must treat like cases alike," states could ban some people from committing physician-assisted suicide while allowing other people to end their lives by refusing life support.[2]

It is important to understand that the Court's rulings did *not* mean that physician-assisted suicide is illegal. The holding meant simply that because the Constitution says nothing about physician-assisted suicide laws, states are free to pass laws that ban *or* legalize physician-assisted suicide. (Five years after the *Glucksberg* and *Quill* decisions, only Oregon had passed a law explicitly legalizing physician-assisted suicide—the Oregon Death With Dignity Act.)

After the *Glucksberg* and *Quill* decisions, it became clear that Michigan had the power to ban Dr. Kevorkian's participation in people's suicides. In fact, Michigan law *did* prohibit assisted suicide. However, rather than backing down, Kevorkian took his actions to the next level. On September 16, 1998, Kevorkian videotaped himself actually injecting a man with a lethal dose of medication, an act for which he was convicted of murder the following year.

Thomas Youk was suffering from amyotrophic lateral sclerosis (ALS, or "Lou Gehrig's Disease"), a debilitating illness that Youk knew would result in a slow and painful death. He wanted to speed up his death to avoid inevitable suffering: He had told his family so and had even made statements to that effect on the videotape. By September of 1998, he had lost a great deal of muscle function, which severely limited his ability to move.

He wanted to die, regardless of the law, and Dr. Kevorkian was willing to "help." He hooked Youk up to an electrocardiogram to monitor his heart rate, and then, unlike past cases in which patients had participated in the operation of the suicide machine or carbon monoxide tank, Dr. Kevorkian decide that he himself "would inject Youk in the vein because 'it is quicker.'"[3] Kevorkian injected Youk first with two chemical sedatives and then with a dose of potassium chloride that stopped his heart. By injecting Youk rather than

THE LETTER OF THE LAW

Michigan's Law on Assisted Suicide

Prohibited acts; violation; penalties...

(1) A person who has knowledge that another person intends to commit or attempt to commit suicide and who intentionally does either of the following is guilty of criminal assistance to suicide, a felony punishable by imprisonment for not more than 4 years or by a fine of not more than $2,000.00, or both:

    (a) Provides the physical means by which the other person attempts or commits suicide.

    (b) Participates in a physical act by which the other person attempts or commits suicide.

(2) Subsection (1) shall not apply to withholding or withdrawing medical treatment.

(3) Subsection (1) does not apply to prescribing, dispensing, or administering medications or procedures if the intent is to relieve pain or discomfort and not to cause death, even if the medication or procedure may hasten or increase the risk of death.

Source: Mich. Comp. Laws §752.1027

allowing the sick man to self-administer the lethal medication, Kevorkian crossed the line between assisted suicide and what many call "voluntary active euthanasia" or "mercy killing."

Kevorkian offered the tape to the television program *60 Minutes*. The sight of Dr. Kevorkian giving a person a lethal injection was disturbing, but the popular news program decided to air portions of the tape anyway, along with an interview with Kevorkian. The tape, watched by viewers around the nation, brought further attention to the debate over whether people have a right to die, an issue that continues to spark debate. In the specific case of Dr. Kevorkian, though, there was little doubt that what he had done was illegal—and prosecutors had a videotape to prove it. A jury convicted Kevorkian in 1999 of second-degree murder, and the Michigan Court of Appeals upheld his conviction in 2001. Although Doctor Death was out of business, the cause he promoted continues to inspire heated debate.

- **Did Dr. Kevorkian's appearance on *60 Minutes* prejudice his case?**

The Debate Continues

Both supporters and opponents of physician-assisted suicide have kept a watchful eye on the situation in Oregon. Few people end their lives under the Oregon Death With Dignity Act. To some, the low utilization proves that physician-assisted suicide is a last resort. To others, even one life taken in this way is too many.

The greatest fear of opponents to physician-assisted suicide

THE LETTER OF THE LAW

From the Fourteenth Amendment:

No state shall make or enforce any law which shall abridge the privileges or immunities of citizens of the United States; nor shall any state deprive any person of life, liberty, or property, without due process of law; nor deny to any person within its jurisdiction the equal protection of the laws.

is that legalization will lead to abuse. They point to abuses in the Netherlands, where the Dutch legal system and medical establishment have long tolerated euthanasia. As became clear in the Kevorkian episode, there is a difference between physician-assisted suicide and euthanasia: In physician-assisted suicide, the patient takes an active step to end his or her life, while in euthanasia, the physician's actions end the patient's life. However, many fear that legalizing physician-assisted suicide will lead to increases in euthanasia.

Studies suggest that a majority of Americans support legalizing physician-assisted suicide,[4] as do a significant percentage of doctors.[5] Yet, the American Medical Association (AMA) continues to oppose the practice, and it is illegal in almost every state. Organizations such as the Hemlock Society, Compassion in Dying, and Death with Dignity work around the nation for legalization, while many doctors' groups, religious denominations, and right-to-life groups work to keep the practice illegal. In the meantime, many people suffer greatly at the end of their lives, some who wish to hasten their deaths, and some who are happy just to be alive. At the same time, evidence suggests that many physicians continue to prescribe medications that relieve pain but also hasten death.

• **Should states ban assisted suicide?**

Each year, many people suffer from terminal illnesses, and some of them want to die quickly and painlessly. However, all states outlaw euthanasia, or "mercy killing," even if the person wants to die. Only Oregon permits physicians to assist terminally ill people in committing suicide, by prescribing lethal doses of medication. Many people in other states also support the practice, though, and numerous states have considered lifting their bans.

People Should Have the Right to Determine When and How They Die

Do people have a "right to die"? Many people say they do, but the U.S. Supreme Court ruled in *Quill* and *Glucksberg* that such a right does not exist under the U.S. Constitution. The Court rejected arguments that abortion rights and the right to refuse medical treatment could be extended to cover decisions to commit suicide. This did not, however, end the debate about the "right to die"—the Court's ruling simply moved the debate to the state legislatures. As the Court concluded in *Glucksberg*:

> Throughout the Nation, Americans are engaged in an earnest and profound debate about the morality, legality, and practicality of physician assisted suicide. Our holding permits this debate to continue, as it should in a democratic society.[1]

In efforts to convince states to legalize physician-assisted suicide, supporters of such legislation offer many of the same arguments offered in the *Quill* and *Glucksberg* cases, asserting that the states, as a matter of policy, should not intrude upon this very personal decision. People who are dying slowly often go through tremendous pain and suffering, and laws prohibiting physician-assisted suicide have the effect of forcing these people to endure their own suffering. For many people, the debate over physician-assisted suicide is really about the right to "death with dignity" without interference from overly restrictive laws.

• **Should the Supreme Court have made a more definitive ruling about physician-assisted suicide?**

Decisions about death are inherently private and not the state's business.

The U.S. Constitution guarantees the people a number of rights. Some are explicitly spelled out in the text of the Constitution, such as the right to vote. Although the Declaration of Independence suggests a right to "life, liberty, and the pursuit of happiness," nowhere does the Constitution mention a right to *die*. Still, over the centuries, the U.S. Supreme Court has held that the Constitution guarantees some rights that are not specifically mentioned in the Constitution. Many of these rights exist under the Fourteenth Amendment to the Constitution, which reads in part: "No state shall . . . deprive any person of life, liberty, or property without due process of law."

In the landmark case of *Roe* v. *Wade*,[2] for example, the U.S. Supreme Court concluded that state laws outlawing abortion violated the due process clause of the Constitution because "liberty" includes a "right to privacy." Relying on past decisions in which it had held that the Fourteenth Amendment protects decisions relating to marriage, contraception, family relationships, and child rearing and education, the

Court held in *Roe* that abortion laws were a similar invasion upon the right to privacy.

Yet, in recent years, the Supreme Court—led by conservative Chief Justice William Rehnquist, with strong support from Justices Antonin Scalia and Clarence Thomas—has been much more reluctant to "discover" rights not explicitly mentioned in the Constitution. Political and religious conservatives have applauded this trend. When in *Quill* and *Glucksberg* supporters of a "right to die" freedom tried to argue that the Fourteenth Amendment creates such a right, the Supreme Court definitively rejected the idea.

• **Should the courts declare rights that are not spelled out in the Constitution?**

Right-to-die supporters had made two major analogies when arguing the case to the Supreme Court, comparing the decision to commit suicide to the decision to have an abortion or to refuse life-sustaining treatment. The organization Compassion in Dying relied on *Planned Parenthood of Southeastern Pa. v. Casey*,[3] which upheld abortion rights, to argue in *Quill*[4] that similar protections should be extended to end-of-life decisions. In *Casey*, it argued, the Court had held that "marriage, procreation, contraception, the decision whether to bear or beget a child, family life and relationships, child rearing, and education" are "central to the liberty protected by the Fourteenth Amendment." Compassion in Dying cited the following passage from the Court's conclusion in *Casey*, as well:

> The mother who carries a child to full term is subject to anxieties, to physical constraints, to pain that only she must bear. . . . Her suffering is too intimate and personal for the State to insist, without more, upon its own vision of the woman's role, however dominant that vision has been in the course of our history and our culture.

Compassion in Dying drew a direct parallel between the "right to die" and other personal rights in the conclusion of its brief in *Quill*:

> To hold that the decision [to commit suicide with the assistance of a physician] is less significant, or less firmly grounded in the Liberty Clause, than the decision whether to bear or beget a child, or to use contraceptives, or to send one's child to private school, would do irreparable damage to this Court's commitment to principled exposition of constitutional rights.

Compassion in Dying also argued that the "right to die" was a logical extension of the right to refuse medical treatment, which had been firmly established in American law. In *Cruzan* v. *Director, Mo. Dept. of Health*, the Supreme Court had held that the Fourteenth Amendment protects the right of competent adults to refuse medical treatment, even life support or other measures necessary to save the patient's life. In *Glucksberg* and *Quill*, right-to-die advocates argued that there should be a similar right to receive treatment that hastens death:

> The person who is dying in intolerable pain or torment faces "suffering [that] is too intimate and personal for the State to insist" that she must bear it. . . .
>
> This is particularly true when suffering occurs in a life already artificially extended . . . through the use of modern technology. The Court recognized this in *Cruzan*, explicitly acknowledging the constitutional liberty of a "seriously ill or dying" patient who is being given food and water by artificial means such as a feeding tube . . . to instruct that such sustenance be withheld in order to hasten death. . . . Just as "[a] seriously ill or dying patient whose wishes are not honored may feel a captive of the machinery required for life-sustaining measures or other medical interventions."[5]

- **What are the differences between rejecting life support and requesting that a physician prescribe a lethal dose of medication?**

Although the Supreme Court rejected the abortion and refusal-of-treatment analogies in *Glucksberg* and *Quill*, right-to-die supporters continue to make the argument that the

FROM THE BENCH

End-of-life Decisions as a "Liberty" Protected by the Constitution

From Justice Stevens's concurring opinion in *Washington* v. *Glucksberg*:

In *Cruzan* . . . the Court assumed that the interest in liberty protected by the Fourteenth Amendment encompassed the right of a terminally ill patient to direct the withdrawal of life sustaining treatment. . . . [This right is] supported by the common law tradition protecting the individual's general right to refuse unwanted medical treatment. . . .

Given the irreversible nature of her illness and the progressive character of her suffering, Nancy Cruzan's interest in refusing medical care was incidental to her more basic interest in controlling the manner and timing of her death. In finding that her best interests would be served by cutting off the nourishment that kept her alive, the trial court did more than simply vindicate Cruzan's interest in refusing medical treatment; the court, in essence, authorized affirmative conduct that would hasten her death. When this Court reviewed the case and upheld Missouri's requirement that there be clear and convincing evidence establishing Nancy Cruzan's intent to have life sustaining nourishment withdrawn, it made two important assumptions: (1) that there was a "liberty interest" in refusing unwanted treatment protected by the Due Process Clause; and (2) that this liberty interest did not "end the inquiry" because it might be outweighed by relevant state interests. . . . I agree with both of those assumptions, but I insist that the source of Nancy Cruzan's right to refuse treatment was not just a common law rule. Rather, this right is an aspect of a far broader and more basic concept of freedom that is decision to commit suicide is a private one in which the states should not have the power to interfere. Their hope is to convince the states that—regardless of the Supreme Court's reading of the Constitution—there are certain inherently private areas of human life that should not be subject to regulation by the states.

The privacy argument was pivotal in the passage of Oregon's

even older than the common law....This freedom embraces, not merely a person's right to refuse a particular kind of unwanted treatment, but also her interest in dignity, and in determining the character of the memories that will survive long after her death. In recognizing that the State's interests did not outweigh Nancy Cruzan's liberty interest in refusing medical treatment, Cruzan rested not simply on the common law right to refuse medical treatment, but—at least implicitly—on the even more fundamental right to make this "deeply personal decision." ...

The now deceased plaintiffs in this action may in fact have had a liberty interest even stronger than Nancy Cruzan's because, not only were they terminally ill, they were suffering constant and severe pain. Avoiding intolerable pain and the indignity of living one's final days incapacitated and in agony is certainly "[a]t the heart of [the] liberty . . . to define one's own concept of existence, of meaning, of the universe, and of the mystery of human life." ...

While I agree with the Court that *Cruzan* does not decide the issue presented by these cases, Cruzan did give recognition, not just to vague, unbridled notions of autonomy, but to the more specific interest in making decisions about how to confront an imminent death. Although there is no absolute right to physician assisted suicide, Cruzan makes it clear that some individuals who no longer have the option of deciding whether to live or to die because they are already on the threshold of death have a constitutionally protected interest that may outweigh the State's interest in preserving life at all costs. The liberty interest at stake in a case like this differs from, and is stronger than, both the common law right to refuse medical treatment and the unbridled interest in deciding whether to live or die. It is an interest in deciding how, rather than whether, a critical threshold shall be crossed.

assisted-suicide law, according to Barbara Coombs Lee, a nurse and attorney:

> [O]ur most vocal support and largest contributions came from people who describe themselves as politically very conservative. They resent a government that interferes in an intensely personal, private decision, and restricts their individual liberty. Many who would oppose a woman's abortion option on the grounds that there is another life to be considered, see no such moral issue in assisted death for terminally ill adults.[6]

Although in the five years after the *Quill* and *Glucksberg* decisions, only Oregon explicitly legalized physician-assisted suicide, right-to-die advocates have had some success advancing the privacy argument in state legislatures. After extensive public hearings, an influential committee in Hawaii's House of Representatives concluded in 2002:

> Your Committee finds it appropriate, compassionate, and humane to authorize a physician to prescribe medication to empower a mentally competent, terminally ill, adult patient, who has a full understanding of options and consequences, to exercise control over this intensely private decision. . . . Your Committee heard pleas to allow individuals who wish to die in peace and dignity to make this decision for themselves, and to live out their years without fear of being forced, at some future time, to continue living in the painful circumstances they have seen others endure.[7]

The assisted-suicide bill did not become law in Hawaii, however, and only time will tell whether the privacy argument is ultimately successful in persuading state legislatures. Many right-to-die supporters firmly believe that if decisions such as abortion, contraception, marriage, and medical treatment are private decisions, then the decision to die with dignity is also a private decision with which the state should not interfere.

Britain's Diane Pretty, shown here with her husband, Brian, is working to reform Britain's assisted-suicide laws. She suffers from a degenerative disease that, while leaving her mind intact, paralyzes her body more severely each year. She intends to end her life when communication with her family is no longer possible, but she is physically incapable of doing this herself. In July of 2001, she asked Britain's director of prosecutions to guarantee that her husband would not be prosecuted for assisting her in suicide. Two years of argument followed, and by March of 2002, when this photograph was taken, the Prettys' case was being heard by the European Court of Human Rights.

People often suffer tremendously because they cannot control their own deaths.

Whether end-of-life decisions are too personal for the state to control or not, their consequences undoubtedly are very serious. Opponents of physician-assisted suicide have argued that decisions involving life and death are of the utmost importance and that the states should therefore be involved, just as the states outlaw certain drugs, require motorcyclists to wear helmets, and regulate hunting safety. The states, opponents say, are involved in many decisions that people might make and in which the states must be involved in order to protect people's lives.

Still, many have raised the question of whether *all* lives are worth saving. Although many opponents of physician-assisted suicide might answer affirmatively, there are certainly cases in which states do not protect lives. Many states sentence convicted criminals to death, and, generally speaking, people are legally permitted to kill other people in self-defense. Where, then, should the line be drawn?

The Hemlock Society, which advocates nationally for the right to die, believes that a line can be drawn. It supports assisted suicide in cases in which "the patient has not more than six months to live," as verified by "at least two independent physicians [who] agree on the diagnosis and the prognosis."[8] In cases such as these, right-to-die advocates argue, physician-assisted suicide is merely hastening a death that is inevitable; because the state cannot *prevent* that death, or even delay it by more than a few months, it should not be empowered to prohibit physician-assisted suicide in such instances.

More significant perhaps than the short duration of time that a person covered by physician-assisted suicide laws would have to live is the quality of his or her life during that brief period of time. The personal testimony of the plaintiffs in *Quill* demonstrates just how profound the suffering of people with terminal illness can be. One woman suffering from incurable cancer testified:

> I have a large cancerous tumor which is wrapped around the right carotid artery in my neck and is collapsing my esophagus and invading my voice box. The tumor has significantly reduced my ability to swallow and prevents me from eating anything but very thin liquids in extremely small amounts. The cancer has metastasized . . . and it is painful to yawn

or cough. . . . In early July 1994 I had the [feeding] tube implanted and have suffered serious problems as a result. . . . I take a variety of medications to manage the pain. . . . It is not possible for me to reduce my pain to an acceptable level of comfort and to retain an alert state.[9]

Another plaintiff, a man suffering from the advanced stages of AIDS, also testified:

In May 1992, I developed a Kaposi's sarcoma skin lesion. This was my first major illness associated with AIDS. I underwent radiation and chemotherapy to treat this cancer. . . . In September 1993, I was diagnosed with cytomegalovirus ("CMV") in my stomach and colon which caused severe diarrhea, fevers and wasting. . . . In February 1994, I was diagnosed with microsporidiosis, a parasitic infection for which there is effectively no treatment. . . . At approximately the same time, I contracted AIDS-related pneumonia. The pneumonia's infusion therapy treatment was so extremely toxic that I vomited with each infusion. . . .

In March 1994, I was diagnosed with cryptosporidiosis, a parasitic infection which has caused severe diarrhea, sometimes producing 20 stools a day, extreme abdominal pain, nausea, and additional significant wasting. I have begun to lose bowel control. . . . For each of these conditions I have undergone a variety of medical treatments, each of which has had significant adverse side effects. . . . While I have tolerated some [nightly intravenous] feedings, I am unwilling to accept this for an extended period of time.[10]

Right-to-die supporters think that it is fundamentally unfair for legislators—who may bear no personal consequences from the legislation—to outlaw physician-assisted suicide and leave others to suffer through the consequences of the ban, as these two people suffered as a result of New York's ban.

- **Do life-and-death decisions belong exclusively to the person whose life is at stake?**

Bans on physician-assisted suicide deny people the opportunity to die with dignity.

No right is absolute, and supporters of the "right to die" recognize that the right must be balanced against the states' interest in preventing death and preserving life. However, right-to-die supporters do argue that in extremely limited cases, the state has nothing to gain by prolonging the lives of people whose death is inevitable; in some cases, all that a person has to look forward to is a few more months filled with unendurable pain. While some people tolerate pain gladly in exchange for the opportunity to spend additional time with their loved ones, other people feel a complete loss of dignity as the pain and the other limitations of their illness make it impossible for them to carry on their lives as they once did.

Throughout history, cultures have had different ways of dealing with death. In many cultures, rituals not only help the dying person find peace, but also help loved ones to deal with the impending death. Many right-to-die supporters believe that bans on physician-assisted suicide interfere with people's innate need to prepare for and face death in their own way. As Barbara Coombs Lee testified before Congress:

> I believe that one reason people . . . choose a hastened death, is because they believe the circumstances of their deaths are very important to the meaning, the story, even the sanctity of their lives. There is something about facing death with courage and grace, with senses intact, that serves their most cherished values and spiritual needs. And I believe, quoting philosopher and legal scholar Ronald Dworkin, that "Making someone die in a way others approve, but he believes a horrifying contradiction of this life, is a devastating, odious form of tyranny."[11]

In addition to cultural and philosophical needs, many people dying of a terminal illness feel a tremendous loss of dignity caused by their physical conditions; they not only feel depleted by their condition but also do not want others to see them as they have become. A coalition of hospice care professionals, quoting a practicing hospice care nurse, highlighted this all-too-frequent loss of dignity in a brief it wrote for *Quill* and *Glucksberg*:

> For many, the pivotal issue is quality of life. Although free of pain, they hate living with the spinal cord compression that left them incontinent of bowel and bladder. Or they hate the inhuman substance that pours from their tumor and onto their clothes, into their hair, onto their furniture. They would rather be dead than live with the brain tumor that has locked them inside a motionless, aphasic body.[12]

Supporters of physician-assisted suicide, whether they call their crusade one for the right to die or one for "death with dignity," hope to convince state legislators that the traditional

• **Is suicide a form of "death with dignity"?**

role of the state in protecting life must take into account the feelings of those whose lives are being "protected."

Despite the Supreme Court's 1997 ruling that physician-assisted suicide is not protected by the Constitution, many supporters of the practice continue to argue that the decision of a competent, terminally ill adult to end his or her own life is an inherently personal decision with which the state should not interfere. The consequences of bans on the practice are needless pain and suffering and a loss of dignity for the terminally ill.

States Should Protect People from Choosing Suicide

P eople and organizations opposing physician-assisted
suicide reject the idea of a "right to die." Often, objections to physician-assisted suicide are based upon religious
teachings that all human life is to be valued, and that any
effort to terminate human life—whether or not the person is
terminally ill—is therefore sinful or immoral. Their efforts
are part of a larger battle for the "right to life": to protect
human life in all forms, including opposing abortion and
stem cell research.

Others have deep-rooted philosophical objections to physician-
assisted suicide. Many people might oppose physician-assisted
suicide even though they support abortion, refusing life support,
stem cell research, or other practices opposed by the "right
to life" movement. Some are opposed to physician-assisted
suicide because they are concerned that choosing suicide is

an irrational choice, motivated by depression or distress rather than carefully weighing the serious consequences of suicide. Others believe that it is simply not possible for physicians to draw a line between lives worth saving and lives not worth saving: Sometimes, even the most pessimistic predictions might be wrong.

Whether the objection to physician-assisted suicide is based in religion or philosophy, opponents believe that the state must ban the practice in order to protect people's lives.

> • Is it possible for doctors to determine which patients will die very soon? What is an acceptable margin of error?
> • Should *all* human life be protected? How can *human life* be defined?

Suicide is different from the types of decisions protected by the Constitution.

Today, in the United States, the right of a woman to have an abortion and the right of an adult to refuse medical treatment are guaranteed by the U.S. Supreme Court's interpretation of the Constitution. Still, opponents of physician-assisted suicide do not want to see these rights extended to a broader right to make life-or-death decisions. Although the Supreme Court refused to extend the right in *Quill* and *Glucksberg*, opponents of physician-assisted suicide continue to face arguments in state legislatures that the states should not be regulating personal decisions relating to death.

Many opponents of physician-assisted suicide do not want to see abortion rights extended to the right to die issue because they oppose abortion as well. A number of religious organizations and other "pro-life" groups oppose both practices because they believe that it is sinful to end any human life—whether it is the life of a four-week embryo or a 95-year-old suffering from a terminal illness. For example, the catechism of the Catholic Church prohibits intentional homicide, abortion, euthanasia, and suicide under the general category of "Respect for Human Life."[1]

Yet, even many abortion supporters oppose physician-assisted suicide, arguing that the two are significantly different. For example, the AMA, which supports the ability of doctors to perform abortions, has argued against physician-assisted suicide. In an amicus brief to the Supreme Court, a coalition of bioethics professors differentiated abortion and physician-assisted suicide by pointing out that abortion is a medical procedure:

> Unlike abortion, assisting a suicide requires no special medical skills or knowledge. Assisting patients to commit suicide is not taught in medical schools, tested on any medical board examinations or discussed in the standard medical texts. . . . Assisting suicide is not a medical procedure, and medicalizing an act runs the risk of making an otherwise unacceptable act appear acceptable.

The professors' brief also pointed out that some of the political aspects of abortion rights were not applicable to physician-assisted suicide:

> A woman's decision whether to have a child determines not only her future relationships with others but her own conception of herself and her role in society. Furthermore, the constitution protects the woman's right in order to ensure that women are treated fairly as free and equal participants in a democracy.[2]

A more challenging analogy frequently mentioned by right-to-die supporters is the right to refuse life-sustaining medical treatment, which the Supreme Court upheld in *Cruzan* v. *Director, Mo. Dept. of Health.* Still, opponents of physician-assisted suicide also have an answer to this question, and they have the authority of the Supreme Court's *Glucksberg* and *Quill* decisions behind them. The Supreme Court explained that the *Cruzan* decision was about refusing unwanted treatment, not about making life-or-death decisions:

> The right assumed in *Cruzan* . . . was not simply deduced from abstract concepts of personal autonomy. Given the common law rule that forced medication was a battery, and the long legal tradition protecting the decision to refuse unwanted medical treatment, our assumption was entirely consistent with this Nation's history and constitutional traditions. The decision to commit suicide with the assistance of another may be just as personal and profound as the decision to refuse unwanted medical treatment, but it has never enjoyed similar legal protection. Indeed, the two acts are widely and reasonably regarded as quite distinct.[3]

Those who oppose state laws that permit physician-assisted suicide can point to the Supreme Court's pronouncement that suicide is not a "fundamental liberty" like abortion and the right to refuse medical treatment.

• **Do legal traditions matter in distinguishing between refusing life support and physician-assisted suicide?**

People are often not competent to make end-of-life decisions.

Opponents of physician-assisted suicide also argue that a "right" has no meaning unless it is exercised freely. Often a court will determine whether a person is competent to make decisions or legally incompetent due to youth, mental retardation, mental illness, dementia, or—as was the case in *Cruzan*—unconsciousness. Although a person has the right to refuse medical treatment, including life support, the Supreme Court has held that "an incompetent person is not able to make an informed and voluntary choice to exercise a hypothetical right to refuse treatment or any other right."[4]

Interestingly, although *Cruzan* is frequently cited as support for the right to refuse treatment, the Supreme Court's ruling in the case was that the state of Missouri could continue to administer life support to Nancy Cruzan, who had been unconscious

FROM THE BENCH

Does the Constitution Protect Physician-Assisted Suicide?

From *Washington* v. *Glucksberg*:

The question presented in this case is whether Washington's prohibition against "caus[ing]" or "aid[ing]" a suicide offends the Fourteenth Amendment to the United States Constitution. We hold that it does not....

We begin, as we do in all due process cases, by examining our Nation's history, legal traditions, and practices.... In almost every State—indeed, in almost every western democracy—it is a crime to assist a suicide. The States' assisted suicide bans are not innovations. Rather, they are longstanding expressions of the States' commitment to the protection and preservation of all human life....

[F]or over 700 years, the Anglo American common law tradition has punished or otherwise disapproved of both suicide and assisting suicide.... In the 13th century, Henry de Bracton, one of the first legal treatise writers, observed that "[j]ust as a man may commit felony by slaying another so may he do so by slaying himself." ... Centuries later, Sir William Blackstone, whose *Commentaries on the Laws of England* not only provided a definitive summary of the common law but was also a primary legal authority for 18th and 19th century American lawyers, referred to suicide as "self murder." ...

[C]olonial and early state legislatures and courts did not retreat from prohibiting assisting suicide. Swift, in his early 19th century treatise on the laws of Connecticut, stated that "[i]f one counsels another to commit suicide, and the other by reason of the advice kills himself, the advisor is guilty of murder as principal." ... And the prohibitions against assisting suicide never contained exceptions for those who were near death. Rather, "[t]he life of those to whom life ha[d] become a burden—of those who [were] hopelessly diseased or fatally wounded—nay, even the lives since a serious accident. Although her family claimed that before her accident she had expressed general wishes not to be kept alive as a "vegetable," she had never formalized these wishes, and the state of Missouri had refused to allow her life support to be removed. The Court agreed with Missouri that the state could require "clear and convincing evidence of the patient's wishes,"[5]

---

of criminals condemned to death, [were] under the protection of law, equally as the lives of those who [were] in the full tide of life's enjoyment, and anxious to continue to live."...

The earliest American statute explicitly to outlaw assisting suicide was enacted in New York in 1828....By the time the Fourteenth Amendment was ratified, it was a crime in most States to assist a suicide....

Though deeply rooted, the States' assisted suicide bans have in recent years been reexamined and, generally, reaffirmed. Because of advances in medicine and technology, Americans today are increasingly likely to die in institutions, from chronic illnesses.... Public concern and democratic action are therefore sharply focused on how best to protect dignity and independence at the end of life, with the result that there have been many significant changes in state laws and in the attitudes these laws reflect. Many States, for example, now permit "living wills," surrogate health care decisionmaking, and the withdrawal or refusal of life sustaining medical treatment.... At the same time, however, voters and legislators continue for the most part to reaffirm their States' prohibitions on assisting suicide.

The Washington statute at issue in this case ... was enacted in 1975 as part of a revision of that State's criminal code. Four years later, Washington passed its Natural Death Act, which specifically stated that the "withholding or withdrawal of life sustaining treatment ... shall not, for any purpose, constitute a suicide" and that "[n]othing in this chapter shall be construed to condone, authorize, or approve mercy killing."...

Attitudes toward suicide itself have changed since Bracton, but our laws have consistently condemned, and continue to prohibit, assisting suicide. Despite changes in medical technology and notwithstanding an increased emphasis on the importance of end of life decisionmaking, we have not retreated from this prohibition.

and allowed the state to keep Cruzan on life support despite her family's objections.

Is someone who wishes to commit suicide legally incompetent to make such an important decision? Many opponents of physician-assisted suicide think so. Although people who wish to commit suicide with the help of a physician must be conscious in order to carry out the act, consciousness does not always equal competence. Opponents of physician-assisted suicide assert that most people who wish to take their own lives are mentally impaired and therefore cannot make a competent decision.

In an article written for *The Atlantic Monthly*, Dr. Ezekiel Emanuel, who specializes in treating cancer, claims that most requests for physician-assisted suicide or euthanasia were motivated by "depression and general psychological distress." He cited studies in which motivating factors included "a perceived loss of dignity . . . fear of a loss of control or of dignity, of being a burden, and of being dependent . . . [and] depression, hopelessness, and having few—and poor-quality—social supports." He concluded that his own experience backed up these studies, writing that "patients who were depressed were most likely to discuss euthanasia seriously, to hoard drugs for suicide, and to have read *Final Exit*, the Hemlock Society suicide manual."[6]

The argument that people contemplating suicide are frequently affected by mental illness, and therefore incompetent to make such an important decision, was accepted by the Supreme Court in its *Glucksberg* and *Quill* rulings. The Court determined in these two cases that physician-assisted suicide was not protected by the U.S. Constitution: "Those who attempt suicide—terminally ill or not—often suffer from depression or other mental disorders. . . . [M]ore than 95% of those who commit suicide had a major psychiatric illness at the time of death; among the terminally ill, uncontrolled pain is a 'risk factor' because it contributes to depression."[7] Opponents of state laws legalizing physician-assisted suicide cite such statistics to argue that suicide is never the "right" decision.

> • **Would a blanket prohibition of physician-assisted suicide resolve the problem that many terminally ill people are depressed?**

States should protect people from making rash end-of-life decisions.

Most opponents of physician-assisted suicide deny that a "right to die" exists. However, they also argue that even if there *were* such a right states still would have ample justification for restricting the exercise of that right. Every constitutional right is subject to some sort of limitation: Freedom of speech does not protect yelling "fire" in a crowded theater, for example, and abortion rights are limited in the later stages of pregnancy. As the Supreme Court explained in *Cruzan*:

> [D]etermining that a person has a "liberty interest" under the Due Process Clause does not end the inquiry; . . . "whether respondent's constitutional rights have been violated must be determined by balancing his liberty interests against the relevant state interests."[8]

Generally, a state has an interest in protecting the lives of its citizens, but supporters of a "right to die" question whether that interest applies in the case of terminally ill people. Among opponents of physician-assisted suicide, many people believe that all human life should be protected, and therefore a blanket ban on the practice is necessary. Other opponents of physician-assisted suicide believe that the state should not be in the business of determining whose life is worth saving and whose is not worth saving; these people believe that a ban on the practice is needed because too many people would take their own lives for the wrong reasons.

Justice David Souter noted in his concurrence in *Glucksberg* that "the lines proposed [for defining an "acceptable" suicide] (particularly the requirement of a knowing and voluntary decision by the patient) would be more difficult to draw than the lines that have limited other recently recognized due process rights."[9] He cited cases in which the Supreme Court had ruled that a state may not ban the sale of contraceptives to married couples, as opposed to unmarried people, and that a state may not ban abortions in the first three months of pregnancy, as opposed to allowing for greater restrictions in the remaining six months.

Where would a state draw the line if it chose to allow physician-assisted suicide? Although groups like the Hemlock Society believe that it is possible to define cases in which the practice could be used, opponents believe that there are too many cases in which people would choose suicide for the wrong reasons. In addition to people whose severe depression renders them incapable of making rational decisions, there might be many other invalid reasons why people might make the decision to end their lives. A commonly cited example is the patient whose treatment is extremely expensive—an ill person who wants to preserve an inheritance for family members, for example, or one whose family actively pressures him or her into accepting death rather than continuing with the expensive treatment. Opponents of physician-assisted suicide believe that financial considerations should not influence a life-or-death decision, and believe therefore that states should prevent opportunities for such decisions to occur. Allowing the practice would simply leave too much opportunity for abuse.

The state also has an interest in preventing the deaths of people who misunderstand the severity of their illness or who do not realize that treatments are available—or will become available. The outlook for cancer patients, and especially AIDS patients, has certainly become more optimistic in recent years.

Nancy Cruzan sustained irreversible brain damage in an automobile accident in 1983. Her parents, Joyce and Joe Cruzan, fought for seven years for the right to end her life, finally winning that right in *Cruzan* v. *Director* (1990). Joe Cruzan, pictured here, began to suffer from severe depression after his daughter's injury, and six years after the legal victory, he himself committed suicide. His death is often pointed to as an indication of the suffering that anti-suicide laws can cause.

In the early years of the AIDS epidemic, the disease was almost always fatal within a short period of time, and people viewed testing positive for the HIV virus as tantamount to a death sentence. Many of the people who supported physician-assisted suicide, including some of the people involved in the *Quill* and *Glucksberg* cases, were people with AIDS. However, today the availability of newer medications makes it possible to live for many years after contracting the HIV virus, which causes AIDS. For example, basketball star Magic Johnson announced in 1991 that he had tested HIV-positive, yet the tenth anniversary of that announcement passed with Johnson in seemingly fine health. People hold out hope that cures will become available for people in the more advanced stages of AIDS.

- **Is the fact that so many people who begin a physician-assisted suicide do not complete it a valid reason to ban the practice?**

People with serious illnesses often experience hopelessness, but their outlooks can change. Experiences in Oregon add support to the idea that people often make requests for physician-assisted suicide but then later change their minds when more aggressive treatment or better palliative care becomes available. Three years after Oregon legalized physician-assisted suicide, *The New England Journal of Medicine* reported that "[s]ubstantive interventions by the physician led many patients to change their minds about assisted suicide."[10] In fact, only 39 percent of patients who requested suicide prescriptions and lived through the mandatory 15-day waiting period actually committed suicide. Opponents point to statistics such as these to suggest that the decision to request physician-assisted suicide is so frequently made irrationally that the state should step in to prohibit the practice.

- **Are there some cases in which recovery can be definitively ruled out?**

Perhaps the strongest arguments that states should regulate physician-assisted suicide come from people who were once thought destined to die. For example, Robert Provan became a successful attorney despite contracting polio at the age of five. A profile released by the National Right to Life Committee describes his situation:

> Due to impairment of respiration and other problems, [his doctors] believed that he would not live to the age of twenty-one. He also might have been a perfect candidate for physician-assisted suicide.

Provan and the committee use his story to argue against the legalization of physician-assisted suicide:

> The tragic consequences of physicians assisting their patients with death would have immeasurable and devastating effects on our culture. According to [Provan], "Many people find a new purpose in their lives in coping with their disease and disabilities. Their struggle even brings new meaning to those who care for them." He adds, "The value of life cannot be destroyed by disease or by disability. Life has a value beyond them."[11]

Opponents of physician-assisted suicide believe that the state must protect the lives of people with terminal illnesses. Some believe that all human lives are sacred and must therefore be protected. Others believe that terminally ill people are especially vulnerable and choose suicide because of depression or for other invalid reasons.

People Should Not Have to Make End-of-Life Decisions Without Medical Advice

People with terminal illness are frequently depressed, and many consider suicide. In this type of situation, a consultation with a medical professional could be extremely helpful. However, because of existing bans on physician-assisted suicide, many patients are afraid to talk to their doctors about suicide. More significantly, the bans can have the effect of causing physicians to withdraw from any discussions about suicide, for fear of criminal liability. Bans on physician-assisted suicide effectively serve as a "gag order" on the subject of suicide, which is an important topic for doctors and patients to be able to discuss.

Lifting bans on physician-assisted suicide would open the dialogue and benefit people with terminal illness, many believe. In the best-case scenario, physicians would be able to provide a thorough assessment of the patients' needs and might be able to prescribe effective palliative or psychiatric care. On the other hand, many supporters of physician-assisted suicide believe that a certain number of patients will want to end their own lives, whether or not a physician participates, and that in these cases regulated suicide is better than unregulated suicide. By establishing a set of procedures for legal suicide, the law can ensure that only people who are truly terminally ill and of sound mind qualify for physician-assisted suicide. The involvement of a physician also offers the opportunity for the act of suicide to be more humane and less traumatic for friends and family.

• **Is it valid to argue that anything that is difficult to regulate should not be regulated? What about guns? Drugs? Speeding?**

Physicians can assess patients seeking assistance with suicide and provide better palliative care or psychiatric referrals.

While opponents of physician-assisted suicide often refer to themselves as "pro-life," people who advocate lifting the bans on the practice are not necessarily "pro-death." In fact, most supporters of legalized physician-assisted suicide would like it to be used in only the most extreme of circumstances. For example, in its brief in *Glucksberg* and *Quill*, the American Medical Students Association (AMSA) took the following position:

> When appropriate palliative care is adequate to relieve the patient's pain and suffering, we do not believe that physician-assisted suicide is an advisable option.[1]

Groups such as AMSA believe that—rather than increasing the number of suicides—legalizing physician-assisted suicide will have the beneficial effect of allowing physicians to discuss suicide with the patients: both the pros *and* the cons. The net result will be that, armed with more honest information, many patients will choose *not* to end their own lives.

- **Should doctors be required to report suicidal patients to the government?**

Dr. Timothy Quill, who was involved in the Supreme Court case that bears his name, writes:

> When a patient expresses a wish to die, this should begin an exploration of the adequacy of palliative care, including assessments of pain management, depression, anxiety, family burnout, and spiritual and existential issues.[2]

A question about suicide serves as an excellent indicator that something is missing from the patient's treatment. Supporters believe that in most cases physicians will be able to respond with better palliative care, psychiatric referrals, or something else that will improve that patient's quality of care, thereby averting suicide.

In the face of criminal penalties for participation in assisted suicide, though, doctors often shy away from any discussion of a patient's wish to die. Dr. Quill took a legal and professional risk by assisting a terminally ill patient with acquiring barbiturates (sleeping pills) that could be used in a suicide. When she called him to request the barbiturates under the guise of needing them to sleep more soundly, he felt that it was his duty as a doctor to talk to his patient.

Dr. Quill's discussion with his patient enabled him to perform two important functions as a physician. He evaluated her mental state, finding that despite her terminal illness it "was clear that she was not despondent and that in fact she was making deep, personal connections with her family and close friends."[3] Had the patient been suffering from depression or

On April 17, 2002, in *Oregon v. Ashcroft*, a federal district judge in Oregon stopped U.S. Attorney General John Ashcroft from blocking Oregon's Death with Dignity Act. Here, James Romney, a former school superintendent who has Lou Gehrig's Disease, speaks to reporters on the steps of a federal courthouse in Portland, Oregon; beside him are two attorneys who argued the case and Eli Stutsman, a co-author of the act. Ashcroft did not attack physician-assisted suicide directly; rather, he attacked the administration of controlled substances.

other forms of distress, Dr. Quill could have provided her with a referral for psychiatric services. Legalizing physician-assisted suicide would make it easier for physicians to have such discussions with their patients rather than fearing the legal consequences. Thus, legalizing the practice could have the effect of increasing the number of terminally ill patients who receive psychiatric care that helps to improve the quality of their remaining days.

Additionally, due to the frankness of his conversation with his patient, Dr. Quill was able to understand his patient's suffering more fully; this made it possible for him to discuss other options, such as hospice and palliative care, more thoroughly:

> As a former director of a hospice program, I know how to use pain medicines to keep patients comfortable and lessen suffering. I explained the philosophy of comfort care, which I strongly believe in.[4]

Although Dr. Quill himself ultimately did not face criminal charges for his role in his patient's death, bans on physician-assisted suicide have a chilling effect on the communication between doctors and patients that is so essential to the provision of proper end-of-life care.

> • **Does it make a difference that Dr. Quill's patient told him that she was having trouble sleeping — that there was a "legitimate purpose" for the prescription as well?**

Carefully regulated physician-assisted suicide provides safeguards for patients.

Before the Supreme Court ruled in 1973 that a decision to have an abortion is protected by the Constitution, many supporters of legalized abortion argued that it was preferable to forcing abortions into "back alleys." Because illegal abortions were widespread and often led to serious health risks or death for women who underwent the procedures, abortion supporters argued that it would be preferable to legalize abortion because the procedure would be much safer if done by physicians with access to medical facilities and with no fear of legal repercussions from transferring patients to emergency rooms if complications arose.

Today, proponents of legalizing physician-assisted suicide make a similar argument. Many believe that the practice is already widespread: Patients ask indirectly for medications that can be used for suicide, and doctors prescribe them. The Hemlock Society's manual, *Final Exit*,[5] and other publications describe to terminally ill people how to commit suicide using prescription drugs. By telling the "right story" to the doctor— for example, about insomnia—the patient might be able to obtain potentially lethal prescriptions. However, out of fear of criminal liability or losing their medical licenses, physicians prescribe the medications for the stated purpose of pain relief or promoting sleep, while concealing their own suspicions that the patients plan to commit suicide.

> • **Should organizations be allowed to publish manuals that tell people how to commit suicide? What about manuals that tell people how to commit murder? Or how to construct a pipe bomb?**

In states where physician-assisted suicide is illegal, if a physician decides to give in to a patient's request for what the physician knows to be a lethal dose of medication, the physician is very unlikely to discuss the decision with his or her colleagues. In such a system, there is very little oversight of whether doctors made the best possible choice in prescribing potentially lethal medications. One brief in *Glucksberg* warned of the potential this lack of oversight creates for abuse:

> Keeping physician-assisted suicide criminal in theory while winking at it in practice creates an environment rife with opportunities for abuse of patients.[6]

By contrast, in Oregon, where physician-assisted suicide is

legal, doctors are able to fully discuss patients' requests for a lethal dose of medications with other colleagues. In fact, under Oregon's Death with Dignity Act, before a physician can prescribe medication for the purpose of assisting suicide, the physician must refer the patient to a second physician, who must verify both that the patient has an incurable, irreversible disease that will result in death within six months and that the patient has made a completely voluntary, informed decision to commit suicide.

Some of the major criticisms of Dr. Kevorkian's actions were that he participated in the deaths of people who were not terminally ill or who had not had proper psychiatric evaluations. In the words of bioethicist Arthur Caplan:

> [T]he range of people that he's been engaged with, is enormously broad and that shook people up. From Janet Adkins, who was told she had Alzheimer's disease, but had minimal symptoms at the time he helped her to die, through . . . people who had a series of disabilities and afflictions but not terminal illness.[7]

By requiring that a physician's participation in suicide be held up to review by another physician, the Oregon law reduces the possibility that a physician will assist in the suicide of someone who is not terminally ill or who is not capable of making an informed decision.

• **How can the law enable doctors to discuss suicide with their patients (and other doctors) without condoning physician-assisted suicide?**

Physicians can keep tragic situations from becoming worse.

Some proponents of physician-assisted suicide believe that a certain number of suicides are inevitable among people with terminal illness. Therefore, they argue, it is better to allow physicians to prescribe a lethal dose of medication to these people, thus allowing for a swift, certain, and painless death, than it is to allow people to attempt suicide on their own.

Trying to devise "safer" methods of suicide might sound illogical, given that the ultimate goal is death. However, proponents of physician-assisted suicide point to at least two ways in which the involvement of physicians can make suicide safer. First, a botched suicide attempt can lead to a great deal of pain before it achieves death—or, worse, end in the patient's survival with new injuries. Second, physician-assisted suicide can have a less traumatic effect on the patient's friends and family than more violent methods of suicide, such as hanging or gunshot.

Arguing in support of physician-assisted suicide in *Glucksberg*, one Washingtonian told the story of what had happened when a terminally ill friend had tried to commit suicide by stockpiling his medication and overdosing on it, an action that he took without a physician's supervision:

> Hugo told me that he had decided to take his own life with some pills he had stockpiled. . . . He prepared two glasses of medication and . . . drank all of one of the glasses. He then . . . passed out before taking the second glass of medication.
>
> Hugo was in a coma for the next several days. I immediately called his physician, who came and examined him. Hugo remained in his home, receiving no food or hydration. Medical personnel told me that Hugo could hear us, even though he was not responding to us.
>
> This was the worst seven days of my life. It was miserable for me, for Hugo, and for others to see his desired death stretched out for so long.

Another person gave a chilling example of what can happen

(continued on page 52)

Procedural Safeguards from the Oregon Death with Dignity Act

Definitions. . . . "Terminal disease" means an incurable and irreversible disease that has been medically confirmed and will, within reasonable medical judgment, produce death within six months. . . .

Attending physician responsibilities.
(1) The attending physician shall:
- (a) Make the initial determination of whether a patient has a terminal disease, is capable, and has made the request voluntarily; . . .
- (c) To ensure that the patient is making an informed decision, inform the patient of:
  - (A) His or her medical diagnosis;
  - (B) His or her prognosis;
  - (C) The potential risks associated with taking the medication to be prescribed;
  - (D) The probable result of taking the medication to be prescribed; and
  - (E) The feasible alternatives, including, but not limited to, comfort care, hospice care and pain control;
- (d) Refer the patient to a consulting physician for medical confirmation of the diagnosis, and for a determination that the patient is capable and acting voluntarily;
- (e) Refer the patient for counseling if appropriate . . .
- (f) Recommend that the patient notify next of kin . . .
- (i) Verify, immediately prior to writing the prescription . . . that the patient is making an informed decision. . . .

Consulting physician confirmation. Before a patient is qualified . . . a consulting physician shall examine the patient and his or her relevant medical records and confirm, in writing, the attending physician's diagnosis that the patient is suffering from a terminal disease, and verify that the patient is capable, is acting voluntarily, and has made an informed decision. . . .

Counseling referral. If in the opinion of the attending physician or the consulting physician a patient may be suffering from a psychiatric or psychological disorder or depression causing impaired judgment, either physician shall refer the patient for counseling. No medication to end a patient's life in a humane and dignified manner shall be prescribed until the person performing the counseling determines that the patient is not suffering from a psychiatric or psychological disorder or depression causing impaired judgment....

Informed decision. No person shall receive a prescription for medication to end his or her life in a humane and dignified manner unless he or she has made an informed decision....

Family notification. The attending physician shall recommend that the patient notify the next of kin of his or her request for medication. . . . A patient who declines or is unable to notify next of kin shall not have his or her request denied for that reason....

Written and oral requests. In order to receive a prescription for medication to end his or her life in a humane and dignified manner, a qualified patient shall have made an oral request and a written request, and reiterate the oral request to his or her attending physician no less than fifteen (15) days after making the initial oral request. At the time the qualified patient makes his or her second oral request, the attending physician shall offer the patient an opportunity to rescind the request....

Right to rescind request. A patient may rescind his or her request at any time and in any manner without regard to his or her mental state. No prescription for medication . . . may be written without the attending physician offering the qualified patient an opportunity to rescind the request....

Waiting periods. No less than fifteen (15) days shall elapse between the patient's initial oral request and the writing of a prescription.... No less than 48 hours shall elapse between the patient's written request and the writing of a prescription....

Construction of Act. Nothing in this Act shall be construed to authorize a physician or any other person to end a patient's life by lethal injection, mercy killing or active euthanasia. Actions taken in accordance with this Act shall not, for any purpose, constitute suicide, assisted suicide, mercy killing or homicide, under the law....

Source: Death with Dignity Act, Or. Rev. Stat. §§127.800-127.897 (2001).

(continued from page 49)

if people who are terminally ill and desperate are left to commit suicide without the assistance of a physician:

> In 1989, my father was dying of lung cancer and was in excruciating pain. . . . We had access to morphine and hinted to him that we could get it for him if he wanted it. However, he refused because he knew it was illegal to assist in a suicide. When he realized that my family was going to be away for a day, he wrote up a beautiful letter, went down to his basement, and shot himself with his 12-gauge shotgun. He was 84. . . . This was a brutal and awful experience for my children and for me. . . . My son-in-law . . . had the unfortunate and unpleasant task of cleaning my father's splattered brains off the basement walls.

Although people who advocate for the legalization of physician-assisted suicide believe that it is a last resort that should not be overused, they believe that, with certain people, the choice of suicide is inevitable. In such cases, it is better to allow a physician to prescribe a lethal dose of medication to ensure that death comes quickly and painlessly, rather than to create more suffering for the patient, friends, and family.

• Can suicide be "painless"?

Advocates of legalizing physician-assisted suicide believe that, whether or not a state bans the practice, a certain number of terminally ill people will attempt suicide and a certain number of physicians will assist their patients' efforts. Therefore, they believe, it is better to regulate the practice and allow doctors to discuss suicide and the alternatives with their patients. This would ensure that those whose suicide is assisted are truly terminally ill and capable of making an informed decision, and would also spare terminally ill people and their families additional suffering from botched or violent suicide attempts.

Widespread Legalization Would Have Devastating Effects on Medical Practice and Research

An important argument against legalizing physician-assisted suicide is that physicians themselves do not support the practice. Despite the efforts of a few doctors who have supported the right to physician-assisted suicide in legal actions and the renegade actions of Jack Kevorkian, the majority of physicians,[1] as well as the organizations that license and represent the interest of physicians, continue to oppose legalization.

Many physicians, and others, are concerned that assisting suicide has never been a part of medical practice, and they would not like to see it made a part of practice. Legalization also poses the threat that suicide will become seen as an acceptable substitute for treatment, which could reduce public support for medical research into cures for serious illnesses. If suicide were to become more acceptable, many worry that minorities, the elderly, and other groups who receive substandard care will be more often pressured into suicide.

> • **Is the participation of physicians necessary for assisted suicide to be humane?**

Assisting suicide is not medicine.

Many physicians are concerned that if more members of their profession begin to participate in suicides, and the practice is legitimized, the integrity of the medical profession will be compromised and people will lose their faith in doctors. Laws in each state regulate the practice of medicine. Additionally, the medical profession, through the AMA and the state medical boards, has established a code of conduct that regulates what a doctor can and cannot do, often placing more restrictions on doctors than the laws on the books do.

The first code of conduct for the medical profession was the Hippocratic Oath. Hippocrates was a physician in ancient Greece who is considered by many to be the "father of medicine," even though medical practice then was certainly vastly different from today's practice. One thing that has not changed is Hippocrates's oath against physician-assisted suicide:

> I will follow that system of regimen which, according to my ability and judgment, I consider for the benefit of my patients, and abstain from whatever is deleterious and mischievous. I will give no deadly medicine to any one if asked, nor suggest any such counsel; and in like manner I will not give to a woman a pessary to produce abortion.[2]

Although for legal and societal reasons, U.S. physicians are no longer barred from performing abortions, the AMA continues to maintain steadfast opposition to physician-assisted suicide in its code of ethics, calling the practice "fundamentally incompatible with the physician's role as healer."[3] In explaining that—regardless of the origins of the Hippocratic Oath—it is still important for physicians to abstain from assisting in suicide, philosophy professor Bernard Baumrin writes:

> It is not merely qua physician that one must not deliberately endanger others under the guise of doing medicine, but that a physician is to be always a champion of life and health. . . . [P]ublic perception binds the practitioner as tightly as an oath.[4]

- **Does the threat of prosecution for assisting suicide have any effect on aggressive efforts to relieve pain?**

Ethics Opinion of the American Medical Association

Physician-assisted suicide occurs when a physician facilitates a patient's death by providing the necessary means and/or information to enable the patient to perform the life-ending act (e.g., the physician provides sleeping pills and information about the lethal dose, while aware that the patient may commit suicide).

It is understandable, though tragic, that some patients in extreme duress — such as those suffering from a terminal, painful, debilitating illness — may come to decide that death is preferable to life. However, allowing physicians to participate in assisted suicide would cause more harm than good. Physician-assisted suicide is fundamentally incompatible with the physician's role as healer, would be difficult or impossible to control, and would pose serious societal risks.

Instead of participating in assisted suicide, physicians must aggressively respond to the needs of patients at the end of life. Patients should not be abandoned once it is determined that cure is impossible. Multidisciplinary interventions should be sought including specialty consultation, hospice care, pastoral support, family counseling, and other modalities. Patients near the end of life must continue to receive emotional support, comfort care, adequate pain control, respect for patient autonomy, and good communication. (I, IV) Issued June 1994 based on the reports "Decisions Near the End of Life," adopted June 1991, and "Physician-Assisted Suicide," adopted December 1993 (*JAMA*. 1992; 267: 2229-33); Updated June 1996.

Source: American Medical Association, Ethics Opinion §2.211, "Physician-Assisted Suicide" (1996), available online at *www.ama-assn.org/ama/pub/category/8459.html*.

In other words, assisting suicide threatens both the moral integrity and the reputation of the medical profession, which is important in maintaining public trust. The medical profession certainly does not want to see a proliferation of "suicide specialists" like Jack Kevorkian. The AMA and state medical boards constantly police physicians, trying to prevent practices that twist the traditional doctor-patient relationship. For example, state medical boards have taken action against doctors who write excessive numbers of prescriptions for painkillers or diet pills, and more recently they have tried to stop the proliferation of Internet sites that offer prescriptions for popular medications such as Viagra without medical consultation.

- **Can the medical profession regulate suicide so as not to create "suicide specialists"?**

Some worry that the image of Dr. Kevorkian as "Doctor Death" makes patients less trusting of their own physicians. Once physicians take over the role of "killer," it is possible that people will begin to fear that their own doctors will pressure them into suicide, or worse yet, euthanize them. In an atmosphere of mistrust, it becomes difficult for doctors to advise their patients, and some patients might even be discouraged from seeking care.

U.S. Attorney General John Ashcroft shares the view that assisting suicide is not part of medical practice. In fact, the attorney general announced his intention to prosecute under federal drug laws any Oregon physician who prescribed a lethal dose of medication under the state's Death with Dignity Act. However, a federal judge in Oregon blocked Ashcroft's efforts in 2002, ruling that the state has the power to define medical practices through its laws, regulations, and medical boards.[5]

The availability of assisted suicide will curtail research on serious illnesses.

One of the major arguments in favor of physician-assisted suicide is that only people who are going to die soon are eligible for a lethal prescription. It is frequently suggested that only a small percentage of people have illnesses that really are incurable. However, this claim begs the question of what could be done to make the percentage of people with incurable illnesses even smaller.

Many people whose illnesses might have been considered incurable a century ago, or even 20 years ago, now have hope for recovery, thanks to advances in the field of medicine. As physician Ezekiel Emanuel points out:

> [D]ecades before the discovery of penicillin (1928) and the development of mechanical respirators (1929), dialysis (1945), and other life-sustaining technologies, serious public discussions of physician-assisted suicide . . . took place . . . in the same language we use today—"patients' rights," "the relief of pain and suffering," "the loss of dignity."[6]

Opponents of physician-assisted suicide question whether these advances would have been made if the approach of the medical community had been to ensure a quick and "painless" death rather than to do whatever was possible to save the patient's life.

- **Would legalizing assisted suicide in the early twentieth century have prevented developments in medicine?**

In the world community, the United States is considered a leader in medical research. Through private donations and federal research funding, physicians and researchers have aggressively pursued research for treatments that will prolong—and improve the quality of—the lives of people suffering from diseases such as various forms of cancer, liver failure, heart disease, respiratory ailments, and many other illnesses. Much of the advancement is the result of dedicated advocacy by individuals suffering from illnesses, as well as groups such as the American Heart Association, American Liver Foundation, and the National Association of People with AIDS.

The first kidney, lung, liver, and heart transplants were performed in the 1960s. Today, many people die while waiting for access to transplantable organs, and health-care advocates believe that more funding is needed. For example, the executive director of the American Liver Foundation testified to Congress:

> The need to increase the rate of organ donation is critical. Today there are more than 74,480 people on the UNOS list waiting for a donated liver, kidney, heart, lung or other organ. . . . [A]bout 17 people die each day while waiting for an organ.[7]

As long as liver transplantation is seen as the only option for people with life-threatening liver diseases, the public will continue to support research and funding into liver transplantation. Opponents of physician-assisted suicide worry that if the practice becomes commonplace, the public will begin to think of assisted suicide as an option for people suffering from these ailments.

Some people with "Lou Gehrig's Disease" favor the legalization of physician-assisted suicide; people with ALS have been among Dr. Kevorkian's "patients." The disease results in progressive loss of muscle function, rendering the patient unable to care for himself or herself, and ultimately results in death. Although many ALS activists hold out hope for a cure, they realize that they are fighting an uphill battle due to the relatively small number of ALS patients compared to people with AIDS, cancer, and heart disease. According to the ALS Association:

> Major biotech and pharmaceutical companies—acutely aware that "only" 30,000 Americans may have ALS at any given time—are reluctant to commit significant funds to the discovery and development of better treatments to combat ALS because they do not anticipate a sufficient financial

return for doing so. And while funding for ALS-specific research by the NIH and other organizations has increased in recent years, much more is needed.[8]

Many ALS activists do not want to see support for ALS research transformed into a belief that suicide is an acceptable option.

The example of AIDS treatment and research provides an excellent example of why it is essential not to prematurely "write off" people's lives. In the early stages of the AIDS epidemic, the disease primarily affected gay men and drug users, and the stigmas surrounding homosexuality and drug use most certainly affected the amount of money dedicated to AIDS research. Eventually, AIDS funding increased, but only after organized efforts by the gay community and AIDS patients and their families.

Ryan White, a teenager from Indiana, became a national

Enforcing Drug Laws Against Oregon Doctors

[T]he Attorney General has determined that assisting suicide is not a "legitimate medical purpose" . . . and that prescribing, dispensing, or administering federally controlled substances to assist suicide violates the Controlled Substances Act [CSA]. Such conduct by a physician registered to dispense controlled substances may "render his registration . . . inconsistent with the public interest" and therefore subject to possible suspension or revocation. . . . The Attorney General's conclusion applies regardless of whether state law authorizes or permits such conduct by practitioners or others and regardless of the condition of the person whose suicide is assisted. . . .

1. *Determination on Use of Federally Controlled Substances to Assist Suicide. . . .* I hereby determine that assisting suicide is not a "legitimate medical purpose" . . . and that prescribing, dispensing, or administering federally controlled substances to assist suicide violates the CSA. . . .
2. *Use of Controlled Substances to Manage Pain Promoted.* Pain management, rather than assisted suicide, has long been recognized as a legitimate

symbol of this struggle. Born with hemophilia, Ryan contracted AIDS from a blood transfusion. After his diagnosis in 1984, Ryan was unable to attend his local public school because of the prevailing prejudices of the time. Although he was told that the disease would be fatal within a short period of time, Ryan and his family fought for his right to attend school, and more broadly, for better care for people with AIDS. Although Ryan died in 1990, his legacy is the Ryan White Care Act,[9] legislation passed later that year that greatly increased funding for services for people with AIDS.

> • Is it wrong to devote less funding to a disease that primarily affects gay men and drug users? Should an illness need a "poster child" to get funding?

Ryan and his family did not give up hope, and most believe it is important that other people with serious illnesses and their

medical purpose justifying physicians' dispensing of controlled substances. There are important medical, ethical, and legal distinctions between intentionally causing a patient's death and providing sufficient dosages of pain medication necessary to eliminate or alleviate pain.

3. *No Change in Current DEA Policies and Enforcement Practices Outside Oregon.* The reinstated determination makes no change in the current standards and practices of the DEA in any State other than Oregon....

4. *Enforcement in Oregon.* Under 3 Oregon Revised Statutes (O.R.S.) §127.855 (1999), an attending physician who writes a prescription for medication to end the life of a qualified patient must document the medication prescribed....

The Department has the authority to take appropriate measures to obtain copies of any such reports or records sent to the Oregon State Registrar....When inspection of these documents discloses prohibited prescription of controlled substances to assist suicide following the effective date of this memorandum, then appropriate administrative action may be taken....

Source: Dispensing of Controlled Substances to Assist Suicide, 21 C.F.R. §1306 (2001).

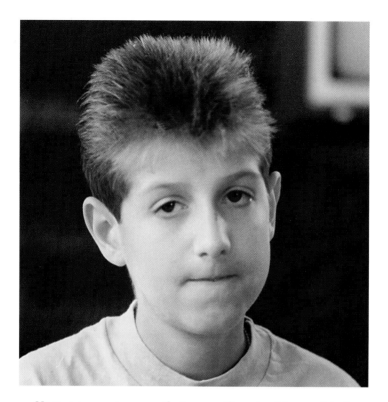

Many opponents worry that promoting physician-assisted suicide as an option for people with terminal illness will lead to an increase in euthanasia and a decrease in funding for research. Ryan White, pictured here in 1988, became a symbol of the fight for better patient care in the early years of the AIDS epidemic. Making suicide an option in cases like his may provide an "easy out" in cases of terminal illness.

families also hold on to hope. Although Ryan's life was not saved, many others have had their lives prolonged and the quality of their lives improved through services made available by the Ryan White Care Act.

Ryan and many other people with AIDS have died after a great deal of suffering, but they fought through that suffering in the hopes of finding a cure for themselves, or at least to provide hope for others with the same illness. Opponents of physician-assisted suicide fear that the widespread legalization of the practice will encourage both doctors and patients to "take the easy way out," and discourage patients from continuing to fight for their lives and the lives of others who suffer the same conditions.

• **Will people with serious illnesses continue to advocate for cures if assisted suicide is legalized?**

Although medical research continues onward, many people will continue to die from serious diseases, but not all of these people are willing to consider suicide as an option, even if a cure is impossible. These people want, and deserve, access to the most advanced palliative care and hospice care that attends to the physical, psychological, and spiritual needs specific to the end of human life. Great advances have been made in pain relief, and hospice care has been developed in response to the public's concerns about the lack of emotional support and comfort in a patient's final days. Opponents of physician-assisted suicide worry that if the public begins to accept suicide as an acceptable option, then improvements in palliative and hospice care will no longer be seen as a priority.

Minorities and the elderly would not receive proper care.

Another major cause of concern for opponents of physician-assisted suicide is that the practice will be disproportionately used on minorities and the elderly. Already, these groups receive substandard health care in the United States. Whether the cause is disparities in funding or physicians' attitudes toward their patients, there are significant differences in the quality of care among people with serious illnesses.

• **If assisted suicide were legal, should there be additional safeguards for minorities and the elderly? If there were, then would the laws be discriminatory?**

According to a fact sheet published in 2000 by the Agency for Healthcare Research and Quality, a federal government agency, minorities are much less likely to receive the best available care for serious illnesses such as heart disease, breast cancer, and HIV/AIDS: African-American people are 13 percent less likely to undergo coronary angioplasty and 33 percent less likely to undergo bypass surgery than are Caucasian people. The length of time between an abnormal screening mammogram and the follow-up diagnostic test to determine whether a woman has breast cancer is more than twice as long in Asian-American, African-American, and Hispanic women as it is in Caucasian women. African Americans with HIV infection are less likely to be on antiretroviral therapy, less likely to receive protection against *Pneumocystis* pneumonia, and less likely to be receiving protease inhibitors than are other persons with HIV.[10] Because minorities are less likely to receive the most aggressive forms of treatment for heart disease, cancer, and AIDS, opponents of physician-assisted suicide are concerned that minorities will be more likely to be diagnosed as "terminally ill" (with no more than six months to live) than Caucasians will be.

> • **Why are there such differences in the ways in which different groups of people are treated for the same disease? Do doctors value some lives less than others?**

Opponents of physician-assisted suicide are especially concerned about the effect that legalization would have on the elderly. A study conducted at Duke University revealed that many elderly patients opposed legalization. This caused Dr. Harold Koenig, the psychiatrist who conducted the study, to fear that if the practice were legalized, some "suicides" would not be voluntary decisions:

[The study] showed that the types of patients most opposed to the idea were those most vulnerable to external influence and who had the least control over their circumstances. These patients generally included women, blacks, poorly educated patients and patients with mild to moderate dementia. . . .

"These findings are provocative and of great concern because the frail elderly, poorly educated and demented members of our society have little power to influence public policy that may directly affect them," Koenig said. "If physician-assisted suicide is made legal, then this population may warrant special protective measures."[11]

Many pro-life organizations share Dr. Koenig's concerns. According to Focus on the Family, a Christian organization that promotes "traditional values":

Social acceptance of physician-assisted suicide tells elderly, disabled and dependent citizens that their lives are not valuable. . . .

Escalating health-care costs, coupled with a growing elderly population, set the stage for an American culture eager to embrace alternatives to expensive, long-term medical care. The so-called "right to die" may soon become the "duty to die" as our senior, disabled and depressed family members are pressured or coerced into ending their lives. Death may become a reasonable substitute to treatment and care as medical costs continue to rise.[12]

Many oppose making assisted suicide a part of medical practice. It conflicts with the physician's traditional role as a healer, and the availability of assisted suicide will necessarily draw support from research cures and pain relief methods. Also, minorities and the elderly already receive substandard health care, and legalized suicide could have a tragic effect on these groups.

Modern Medicine Has Increased the Need for Physician-Assisted Suicide

Advocates of physician-assisted suicide, including many physicians, reject the idea that the practice is incompatible with the responsible practice of medicine. Perhaps assisted suicide conflicted with the traditional practice of medicine, but medical science has changed drastically in recent years. The average lifespan in the United States is now approximately 77 years—a dramatic change from the beginning of the twentieth century, when it was under 50 years.[1] Some people think that medicine has gone too far: Often, people's lives are extended for years beyond the point at which they are able to care for themselves or even recognize their loved ones.

Supporters of physician-assisted suicide do not think that it should be a preferred option; nor, they argue, does it replace or interfere with medical research into curing disease or developments in pain relief. However, they contend that the practice is a necessary complement to artificially extending lives, and that it is really not that different from current medical practices, such as withdrawing life support or providing pain relief medications that hasten death.

The result of medical research is that people live past the stage at which they can enjoy life.

People and organizations advocating for the legalization of physician-assisted suicide believe that medicine has changed drastically. Advances in medicine have prolonged and improved the lives of many people: There is new hope for people diagnosed with cancer, heart disease, and many other ailments that once had a much higher mortality rate. Yet, while many people have benefited from medical science, assisted-suicide advocates believe that with the improvements have come undesirable results for some people. The controversial "Doctor Death," Jack Kevorkian, writes:

> In quixotically trying to conquer death, doctors all too frequently do no good for their patients' "ease"; but at the same time, they do harm instead by prolonging and even magnifying patients' dis-ease.[2]

For some people with chronic diseases, medical treatments have kept them alive, but in great pain, unable to do any of the activities that they once enjoyed. As people live longer, many begin to suffer from dementia or the memory loss associated with Alzheimer's disease and might not even recognize loved ones. People frequently outlive their spouses for many years, and some lose contact with all friends and family, spending years of isolation in nursing homes. There can be a tremendous emotional burden for the families of people whose lives are sustained artificially for years while their quality of life continues to deteriorate.

The resulting medical bills can also create financial burdens for families. As people age, their medical expenditures increase drastically. Data collected by the Federal Interagency Forum on

Aging-Related Statistics about Medicare beneficiaries indicate that health-care expenditures for people aged 85 or older are 77 percent higher than are those for people between the ages of 65 and 69.[3] The brash Dr. Kevorkian has criticized "medicine's misguided commitment to maintaining life at all costs (which comprises a fairly large chunk of our gross national product)."[4]

> • **Is it a problem that people are living longer than they did in the past? What are the advantages and disadvantages of this?**

Although few moderate supporters of physician-assisted suicide would suggest that it is possible to place a value on human life, society does have a limited amount of money to spend on health care, and many people would like to see more money spent on preventive care, rather than on treating terminal illnesses. However, based on experience in Oregon, it does not appear that poor people will be coerced into choosing suicide because of economic pressures: Of the 21 patients who ended their lives legally in 2002, all had health insurance, and 8 were college graduates.[5]

Recognizing that medicine has developed the technology to keep people alive long after the desire to live has gone, states have enacted "living will" laws that allow people to plan in advance to refuse life-sustaining treatment such as feeding tubes and artificial respiration. However, assisted-suicide advocates think that "living will" laws are not enough because they are of no use to people who are suffering from a painful, terminal disease but are not being sustained by life support.

In Washington, the Natural Death Act allows people to refuse medical or surgical treatments that could prolong life; however, assisting suicide remains a felony. In the *Glucksberg* case, the Compassion in Dying organization challenged this seeming contradiction in Washington's law. The group claimed that, as a result of the ban on physician-assisted suicide:

A person who is suffering intolerably while dying, having been brought to this point by chemotherapy, an organ trans-

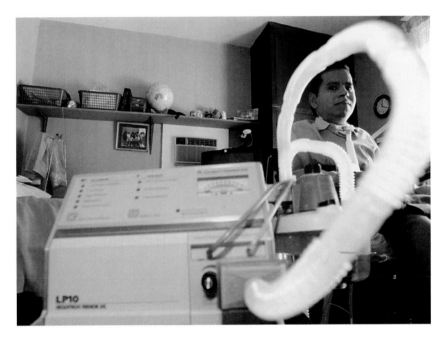

The question of physician-assisted suicide has become more important as the technology that prolongs life has advanced. Many patients now find themselves unable to live without machines that restrict their movements and often cause different kinds of pain, and some may prefer not to live at all. This man, Marcelino Barrientes, has multiple sclerosis. High summer temperatures around his Wisconsin home in 1997 forced him to buy a portable electric generator; for him, even a brief heat-related power outage could be fatal.

plant, or some other technological advance, may well during her artificially prolonged death "feel a captive" of the State within the prison house of her own body.[6]

Many people feel that this "prison house" is imposed by a system of laws imposed by religious beliefs that not all citizens share. In fact, national polls indicate that 65 percent of Americans favor legalizing physician-assisted suicide.[7] Kevorkian has criticized "the inflexible and harshly punitive Judeo-Christian dogma that espoused the inviolable 'sanctity' of human life," calling laws against physician-assisted suicide and euthanasia "arbitrary" in light of "social, demographic, economic, and social changes."[8] Although Kevorkian's support of euthanasia is repugnant to some supporters of physician-assisted suicide, other more moderate supporters have also criticized a prohibition that they feel is rooted in doctrine. For example, Raphael Cohen-Almagor writes, "The view that holds that we should always preserve life no matter what patients want . . . is morally unjustifiable."[9]

> • **Is the answer to rising medical costs to increase spending, or to cut services to certain groups of people?**

Physician-assisted suicide is compatible with palliative care and medical research.

Although opponents of physician-assisted suicide charge that legalizing the practice will discourage medical research and the development of palliative care options, supporters dispute this claim. Some have suggested that palliative care will be unaffected by the legalization of physician-assisted suicide, because one is not a substitute for the other:

> Those who face death may not be troubled by the prospect of pain. . . . More often they are troubled by the prospect of loss of dignity as they define it, isolation, loneliness, [and] fear.[10]

In fact, some supporters believe that legalization of physician-assisted suicide might even result in *more* research into palliative care. For example, the Oregon group Death with Dignity contends:

> Strides in end-of-life care have also meant more attention to pain management. . . . The Joint Commission on Accreditation of Healthcare Organizations (JCAHO) instituted new pain control standards in January 2001.[11]

Although it seems contradictory to think that the availability of physician-assisted suicide would lead to the development of better care for the dying, advocates have long made the argument that the entire system of care for people with terminal illnesses needs reform. Groups like Compassion in Dying and Death with Dignity not only call for the legalization of physician-assisted suicide, but also for more compassion by doctors and a greater understanding of the needs of people with terminal illnesses. By calling attention to the difficulties that lead people to choose suicide, the medical community can respond by developing alternatives to suicide.

Sometimes, doctors offer treatments—such as chemotherapy, radiation therapy, or surgeries—that have little probability of saving a person's life, but have the undesirable effect of causing additional suffering. In reaction to such practices, the concept of hospice care was developed to comfort a person with a terminal illness rather than putting him or her through futile attempts at a cure. Some hospice and palliative care professionals have

THE LETTER OF THE LAW

Washington's Criminal Penalties for Physician-Assisted Suicide

Promoting a suicide attempt.
(1) A person is guilty of promoting a suicide attempt when he knowingly causes or aids another person to attempt suicide.
(2) Promoting a suicide attempt is a class C felony.

Maximum sentences for crimes committed July 1, 1984, and after.
(1) Felony. No person convicted of a classified felony shall be punished by confinement or fine exceeding the following: ... For a class C felony, by confinement in a state correctional institution for five years, or by a fine in an amount fixed by the court of ten thousand dollars, or by both such confinement and fine.

Source: Wash. Rev. Code §§9A.20.021, 9A.36.060 (2002)

argued that assisted suicide should be an option within the range of services offered to help a person "die well":

> Hospice care developed out of a sense of frustration with the treatment of the dying, and as a reaction against the abuses of an impersonal high-technology approach to patients. . . . Patient autonomy, personal choice and reclaiming control in one's final days of life have always been central to hospice philosophy. . . . Helping a terminally ill patient die at his or her request is at one end of the continuum of lifelong medical care when healing becomes impossible—as it does in every life.[12]

Similarly, advocates also contest claims that the availability of physician-assisted suicide will curtail medical research. The main reason why legalization of physician-assisted suicide will not negatively impact the progress of medical research into cures for serious illness is that suicide is always seen as a last resort. In fact, in Oregon, where physician-assisted suicide is legal, only 21 people ended their lives under the law in 2001, according to a state Department of Human Services report, compared to approximately 30,000 deaths annually in the state.

• **Is it possible to determine how nationwide legalization of physician-assisted suicide would affect research, based on the effect of Oregon's legalization?**

Most people will continue to fight their illnesses, and they and their families will continue to demand that research be done into finding cures. Still, according to groups like Compassion in Dying, for a small number of people the option of suicide must be available:

> In many of our religions and cultures, bearing such suffering at the end of life is seen as an "ennobl[ing]" act, involving pain that should (or indeed must) be borne "with . . . pride." . . . Many of us would never choose to take life-ending drugs, even were we terminally ill, debilitated and suffering intolerably on the edge

of death. Nonetheless, in the United States the decision whether to die a death marked by such suffering must, to the degree fate and medicine permit, be left to the individual.[13]

Physician-assisted suicide is not a significant change from current medical practice.

Although the AMA, state medical boards, and various other medical societies oppose physician-assisted suicide, almost half of U.S. physicians believe that the practice should be permitted, according to a study published in *Medical Economics*, and a majority of physicians under the age of 45 support legalization.[14] Although these results might seem surprising, many supporters believe that physician-assisted suicide is not really that much different from current practices of the medical profession, some of which are not only legal, but are considered ethical obligations of doctors.

Opponents of physician-assisted suicide try to distinguish it from the withdrawal of life support by describing the latter as a passive approach: In essence, they claim, the doctor is doing nothing to cause the patient's death; rather, the death is occurring naturally. However, withdrawing life support does require a series of affirmative acts, according to the American Medical Students Association:

[T]o disconnect a respirator, a physician or nurse must take each of the following steps:

1. turn off the respirator;
2. disconnect the machine from the tube that goes to the patient's lungs;
3. remove the tube from the patient's lungs;
4. administer morphine or barbiturates to ease the patient's sense of suffocation; and
5. monitor medication levels to ensure that symptoms of severe air hunger do not arise.

- **Do the relative amounts of involvement in withdrawing life support and assisting suicide make the two actions similar?**

Although the Supreme Court, in *Quill* and *Glucksberg*, rejected arguments that physician-assisted suicide is no different from withdrawing life support, the two are remarkably similar.

Washington's "Natural Death Act" Allowing Withholding of Life Support

Legislative findings.

The legislature finds that adult persons have the fundamental right to control the decisions relating to the rendering of their own health care, including the decision to have life-sustaining treatment withheld or withdrawn in instances of a terminal condition or permanent unconscious condition.

The legislature further finds that modern medical technology has made possible the artificial prolongation of human life beyond natural limits.

The legislature further finds that, in the interest of protecting individual autonomy, such prolongation of the process of dying for persons with a terminal condition or permanent unconscious condition may cause loss of patient dignity, and unnecessary pain and suffering, while providing nothing medically necessary or beneficial to the patient. The legislature further believes that physicians and nurses should not withhold or unreasonably diminish pain medication for patients in a terminal condition where the primary intent of providing such medication is to alleviate pain and maintain or increase the patient's comfort....

In recognition of the dignity and privacy which patients have a right to expect, the legislature hereby declares that the laws of the state of Washington shall recognize the right of an adult person to make a written directive instructing such person's physician to withhold or withdraw life-sustaining treatment in the event of a terminal condition or permanent unconscious condition. The legislature also recognizes that a person's right to control his or her health care may be exercised by an authorized representative who validly holds the person's durable power of attorney for health care....

Both require a set of actions by a doctor or other health-care professional, and both result in the death of someone who would otherwise live. In fact, withdrawing life support requires much more involvement with the patient than does physician-assisted suicide, which requires the doctor only to write a prescription, leaving the ultimate decision and act of suicide to the patient.

Definitions....

(5) "Life-sustaining treatment" means any medical or surgical intervention that uses mechanical or other artificial means, including artificially provided nutrition and hydration, to sustain, restore, or replace a vital function, which, when applied to a qualified patient, would serve only to prolong the process of dying....

(9) "Terminal condition" means an incurable and irreversible condition caused by injury, disease, or illness, that, within reasonable medical judgment, will cause death within a reasonable period of time in accordance with accepted medical standards, and where the application of life-sustaining treatment serves only to prolong the process of dying....

Procedures by physician....

(1) Prior to the withholding or withdrawal of life-sustaining treatment from a qualified patient pursuant to the directive, the attending physician shall make a reasonable effort to determine that the directive complies with [the law] and, if the patient is capable of making health care decisions, that the directive and all steps proposed by the attending physician to be undertaken are currently in accord with the desires of the qualified patient....

(3) The directive shall be conclusively presumed, unless revoked, to be the directions of the patient regarding the withholding or withdrawal of life-sustaining treatment....

Mercy killing or physician-assisted suicide not authorized.

Nothing in this chapter shall be construed to condone, authorize, or approve mercy killing or physician-assisted suicide, or to permit any affirmative or deliberate act or omission to end life other than to permit the natural process of dying....

Source: Wash. Rev. Code §§70.122.010-70.122.100 (2002)

Not only is the removal of life support allowable under current law—under Washington's Natural Death Act and similar laws in other states, patients have the right to *insist* that life support be withdrawn. The Supreme Court has even held that "a competent person has a constitutionally protected liberty interest in refusing unwanted medical treatment."[15] Further, doctors have an ethical obligation to comply with their patient's wishes in withdrawing life support:

> The principle of patient autonomy requires that physicians must respect the decision to forgo life-sustaining treatment . . . [including] mechanical ventilation, renal dialysis, chemotherapy, antibiotics, and artificial nutrition and hydration.[16]

• Is there a difference between a "living will" rejecting life support and a decision to commit suicide?

Another medical practice with which physician-assisted suicide shares many similarities is "terminal sedation," or providing high doses of pain medication to dying patients, even though the same medication that relieves their pain might also lead to a quicker death. For example, a family doctor from Texas told *Medical Economics*:

> I'd have a hard time personally and ethically giving someone a lethal dose of medication. . . . But I wouldn't have a problem giving increasing doses of morphine until pain is relieved, knowing full well I'm subjecting the patient to some risk of death.[17]

In fact, while opposing physician-assisted suicide, AMA policy requires physicians to provide "effective palliative care even though it may foreseeably hasten death."[18]

• Can prescribing high doses of medication be compared to firing a gun into a crowd of people?

For opponents of physician-assisted suicide, there is a clear distinction between actions designed to result in death and actions that have a high likelihood of resulting in death. The difference lies in the physician's state of mind. However, supporters of legalizing physician-assisted suicide believe that the distinction is an imaginary one: Doctors know that they are hastening death, no matter what their stated intentions are. The law does not distinguish between shooting at someone in order to kill him or her and firing a gun into the crowd of people, knowing that it is most likely that someone will be killed. Therefore, supporters reason, there should be no legal difference between terminal sedation and assisted suicide.

- **Why does the American Medical Association prohibit assisting suicide if so many doctors support it?**

The practice of medicine has changed dramatically in the last century, and some believe that physician-assisted suicide is a necessary component of change. People are living much longer lives, and although further research into curing disease and relieving pain is important, giving people control over the end of their lives is also important, and not really a significant change from current practices.

Nothing Justifies Taking a Human Life

S upporters of physician-assisted have come up with a
number of reasons why physician-assisted suicide is
desirable or necessary. Yet, opponents believe that none of
these explanations justifies taking a human life and that many
of the reasons why people support legalization are in fact
strong arguments *against* legalization.

To many, no ideas of liberty, privacy, convenience, or
economics can overcome the basic belief that killing people is
wrong and that the government should not condone it in
any form. Regardless of how the practice is described, many
fear that legalizing physician-assisted suicide is simply a step
toward systematically eliminating the elderly and disabled,
whether they choose death or not.

Physician-assisted suicide violates historical and contemporary beliefs.

Although supporters of physician-assisted suicide cite statistics that indicate that a majority of Americans generally support physician-assisted suicide, opponents believe that these statistics do not tell the whole story. For many of the people who respond to such polls, the question is simply an abstract question with little impact on their lives. However, among older adults, who are more likely to face a terminal illness than younger people, support decreases. In fact, a poll conducted by the American Association of Retired Persons (AARP) in 2000 found that support for physician-assisted suicide decreases with age. Although 53 percent of people between the ages of 45 and 54 supported legalization, only 35 percent of those aged 75 and older did. As research scientist Powell Lawton explained in the AARP-sponsored magazine *Modern Maturity*:

> Social attitudes toward physician-assisted suicide . . . are heavily colored by the denial among younger people that . . . they would be willing to accept a partial life. . . . [Older adults] have already had some trying times to deal with, and they've developed new frames of reference by which to judge their lives.[1]

> • **Why does support for physician-assisted suicide seem to decline with age — "old-fashioned" values, or fear of abuse?**

Some supporters of physician-assisted suicide argue that objections are based either on religious values that not all people share or on obsolete belief systems. Although many oppose physician-assisted suicide on religious grounds, there are also substantial historical precedents for the bans, as well as a number of nonreligious reasons for objecting to the practice of empowering physicians to assist in people's deaths.

For example, many believe that social justice requires a ban on physician-assisted suicide in order to guarantee that all people are treated equally, as required by the Constitution. People with disabilities, for example, have organized a civil rights movement similar to the women's movement or the African-American civil rights movement. Many people

FROM THE BENCH

Do States Have an Interest in Preventing All Suicides?

From *Washington* v. *Glucksberg*, 521 U.S. 702 (1997):

Washington has an "unqualified interest in the preservation of human life."...The State's prohibition on assisted suicide, like all homicide laws, both reflects and advances its commitment to this interest...."[T]he interests in the sanctity of life that are represented by the criminal homicide laws are threatened by one who expresses a willingness to participate in taking the life of another."...

The Court of Appeals also recognized Washington's interest in protecting life, but held that the "weight" of this interest depends on the "medical condition and the wishes of the person whose life is at stake."...Washington, however, has rejected this sliding scale approach and, through its assisted suicide ban, insists that all persons' lives, from beginning to end, regardless of physical or mental condition, are under the full protection of the law. . . . As we have previously affirmed, the States "may properly decline to make judgments about the 'quality' of life that a particular individual may enjoy,"...This remains true...even for those who are near death.

Relatedly, all admit that suicide is a serious public health problem, especially among persons in otherwise vulnerable groups....The State has an interest in preventing suicide, and in studying, identifying, and treating its causes....

The State also has an interest in protecting the integrity and ethics of the medical profession.... And physician assisted suicide could, it is argued, undermine the trust that is essential to the doctor patient relationship by blurring the time honored line between healing and harming....

Next, the State has an interest in protecting vulnerable groups—including the poor, the elderly, and disabled persons—from abuse, neglect, and mistakes....We with disabilities oppose physician-assisted suicide on the grounds of fairness. According to the disability group Not Dead Yet:

This disability opposition is not based on any religious perspective. . . . In fact, our opposition to legalization of assisted

have recognized ... the real risk of subtle coercion and undue influence in end of life situations. . . . Similarly, the New York Task Force warned that "[l]egalizing physician assisted suicide would pose profound risks to many individuals who are ill and vulnerable. . . . The risk of harm is greatest for the many individuals in our society whose autonomy and well being are already compromised by poverty, lack of access to good medical care, advanced age, or membership in a stigmatized social group." . . . "[A]n insidious bias against the handicapped—again coupled with a cost saving mentality—makes them especially in need of Washington's statutory protection." . . . If physician assisted suicide were permitted, many might resort to it to spare their families the substantial financial burden of end of life health care costs.

The State's interest here goes beyond protecting the vulnerable from coercion; it extends to protecting disabled and terminally ill people from prejudice, negative and inaccurate stereotypes, and "societal indifference." . . . The State's assisted suicide ban reflects and reinforces its policy that the lives of terminally ill, disabled, and elderly people must be no less valued than the lives of the young and healthy, and that a seriously disabled person's suicidal impulses should be interpreted and treated the same way as anyone else's. . . . [Euthanasia and assisted suicide send] negative messages ... to handicapped patients. . . .

Finally, the State may fear that permitting assisted suicide will start it down the path to voluntary and perhaps even involuntary euthanasia. . . . [T]he "decision of a duly appointed surrogate decision maker is for all legal purposes the decision of the patient himself," ... [and] "in some instances, the patient may be unable to self administer the drugs and ... administration by the physician ... may be the only way the patient may be able to receive them," ... and that not only physicians, but also family members and loved ones, will inevitably participate in assisting suicide. . . . Thus, it turns out that what is couched as a limited right to "physician assisted suicide" is likely, in effect, a much broader license, which could prove extremely difficult to police and contain. . . . Washington's ban on assisting suicide prevents such erosion.

suicide is that it violates our right to equal protection of the law, and violates the Americans With Disabilities Act, to set up a double standard for the manner in which society responds to suicidal people, a two-tiered system whereby some people are given suicide intervention and others are given suicide assistance.[2]

Not Dead Yet's major concern about physician-assisted suicide is that people with disabilities will be systematically "eliminated" by the practice. These fears are well grounded in recent history. In Germany, for example, even before the Nazi regime, physicians participated in the killing of people with disabilities, a practice that became widespread under Adolf Hitler.

For many years, the Netherlands has tolerated euthanasia and physician-assisted suicide, subject to certain guidelines. However, writes Margaret Somerville, in many cases even the Dutch medical guidelines are ignored: "Some (probably many) of these cases have occurred," she writes. ". . . These cases included not only incompetent adults but also handicapped newborn babies."[3]

The problems associated with the system of euthanasia in the Netherlands did not escape the notice of the Supreme Court in *Glucksberg*:

This concern is further supported by evidence about the practice of euthanasia in the Netherlands. The Dutch government's own study revealed that in 1990, there were 2,300 cases of voluntary euthanasia (defined as "the deliberate termination of another's life at his request"), 400 cases of assisted suicide, and more than 1,000 cases of euthanasia without an explicit request. In addition to these latter 1,000 cases, the study found an additional 4,941 cases where physicians administered lethal morphine overdoses without the patients' explicit consent. . . . This study suggests that, despite the existence of various reporting procedures, euthanasia in the Netherlands has not been limited to competent, terminally ill adults who are enduring physical suffering, and that regulation of the practice may not have prevented abuses in cases involving vulnerable persons, including severely disabled neonates and elderly persons suffering from dementia.[4]

• **Does the Netherlands' experience with euthanasia indicate what would happen if the United States legalized physician-assisted suicide?**

Economics and convenience do not justify taking human lives.

Some of the reasons why some people argue for legalizing physician-assisted suicide are the same reasons why other people believe that prohibiting it is absolutely necessary. Supporters argue that physician-assisted suicide has become necessary in light of increasing life expectancies and rising medical costs. However, opponents of legalization reject arguments that medical science prolongs anyone's life "too long" or that the cost of medical bills can be a valid reason to "pull the plug."

Arguments about costs and "showing mercy" to the old are particularly dangerous and pose a great potential for abuse. Many believe that families of terminally ill people would collude with doctors to pressure a patient into choosing suicide: Although the family might convince the doctor that suicide is "what is best" for the patient, the family's real motivation could be financial.

On a larger scale, physician-assisted suicide poses threats in a health-care system driven to cut costs. For some, one of the main reasons to continue to prohibit physician-assisted suicide is the movement of American health care to a system of managed care. Historically, doctors and their patients made decisions as to the care that was necessary, and insurance companies reimbursed doctors for service to policyholders. However, as health-care costs began to rise dramatically, some providers of health insurance began to take a more active role in deciding what services are covered. Many managed care organizations, such as health maintenance organizations (HMOs) require people to visit a specific doctor for referrals to services and require prior authorization for expensive services, such as surgery or hospitalization.

The goal of HMOs and other managed-care organizations is to make money by reducing health-care costs. They often use a "capitation" system, under which a doctor or a hospital is paid a certain amount for providing services to each person, regardless of which services are provided or how often. Many people criticize such arrangements, saying they create incentives for doctors to provide fewer services: Because a doctor or a hospital is paid the same regardless of what the doctors do, the doctor will make a greater profit from patients for whom she provides fewer services. In other managed-care arrangements, in which doctors are reimbursed for each particular service, some doctors fear that they will lose their contracts if they provide too many expensive services.

- **How can abuses by managed-care companies be prevented?**

Because providing a lethal prescription is much less expensive than the hospitalizations, life support, surgeries, or other treatment often associated with terminal illnesses, opponents of physician-assisted suicide fear that managed care will encourage suicides. For example, doctors might go along with their patient's wishes even if the doctor thinks that the patient is depressed. Or the doctor might even encourage the patient to choose suicide rather than expensive treatments.

There is a danger, because managed care encourages doctors to spend less time with patients, that even well-meaning physicians would be pressured to encourage suicide among patients. Bioethicist John Annas writes:

> Expert palliative care no doubt is an expensive and time-consuming proposition. . . . It is highly doubtful that the context of physician-patient conversation within this new dispensation of "turnstile medicine will be at all conducive to human decisions untainted by subtle economic coercion.[5]

Legalizing physician-assisted suicide is a slippery slope.

One of the most frequently stated objections to physician-assisted suicide is that it creates a legal "slippery slope." The term "slippery slope" is used in logic and legal reasoning, and can perhaps be best summed up by the common phrase, "Give 'em an inch, and they'll take a mile." Opponents believe that legalization of physician-assisted suicide will lead to greater evils. If the law allows competent, terminally ill adults to end their own lives with the assistance of a physician by taking a lethal dose of medication, then it will only be a matter of time before the law allows euthanasia—for example, a physician giving a competent patient a lethal injection of medication. And then the law will allow a physician to give a lethal injection to an incompetent patient: a person in a coma, or a person whose dementia has made a competent decision impossible. Next, the law will allow for euthanasia of people who are not terminally ill, such as children with birth defects. Of course, this "slippery slope" is not the only possible course of events— it may not even be probable—and supporters of legalizing physician-assisted suicide believe that this can be done without opening a Pandora's box.

The case of Regina Pullum, shown here in 2002, illustrates an argument against physician-assisted suicide. Her son Dallas was involved in an accident in April of 2000, and she and her husband later faced the difficult decision of whether to end his life support. Their other son pleaded with them to postpone the decision even a little while; they did, and Dallas emerged from his coma. Opponents to suicide argue that cases like this may be common, that grieving relatives, even with the best intentions, may give up hope too soon.

But there is an important difference between the American legal system and the abstract study of logic, and in the context of physician-assisted suicide, the "slippery slope" to euthanasia is a very real danger. It is possible to argue that states are constitutionally barred from legalizing physician-assisted suicide without legalizing euthanasia. This legal challenge would be based upon the equal protection clause of the Fourteenth Amendment, which, once again, forbids any state to "deny to any person within its jurisdiction the equal protection of the laws."

Although the original purpose of the equal protection clause—which was enacted at the end of the Civil War—was to prevent states from discriminating based on skin color or ethnic background, courts have held that the clause prohibits discrimination against other groups of people—for example, immigrants, war veterans, and people with disabilities. In fact, in the past, advocates of legalizing physician-assisted suicide have argued that the states should not be allowed to discriminate against people who are terminally ill but do not require life support in order to stay alive. In the *Glucksberg* case, the organization Compassion in Dying argued that the state of Washington violated the equal protection clause:

> The State . . . distinguishes between [1] those competent, terminally ill adults whose condition requires life-sustaining treatment and [2] those whose condition does not. The first group has the right to direct the course of treatment with the specific purpose and result of hastening death. The second group does not, and must suffer the very same pain and suffering and loss of dignity and privacy from which the statute and common law protect the first group.[6]

• **Should people have "equal protection" rights outside of protection from discrimination by race or gender?**

Although the Court rejected this particular equal protection argument in *Quill*, it made its decision based on the principle that the cause of death is different: "[W]hen a patient refuses life sustaining medical treatment, he dies from an underlying fatal disease or pathology; but if a patient ingests lethal medication prescribed by a physician, he is killed by that medication."[7] In both situations, though, physician-assisted suicide and euthanasia the cause of death is the medication. Therefore, there is a very real probability that in Oregon—or in other states that decide to grant people a right to physician-assisted suicide—the law must be extended to grant a "right" to euthanasia.

One example of this is a person who is terminally ill, is not depressed, and is fully capable of making an informed decision, but is so physically disabled that he or she cannot take medication without help. Because Oregon's law allows a physician to prescribe a lethal dose of medication but does not allow the doctor to *administer* that medication, a physician could not legally help such a person to end his or her life. This person could bring a lawsuit claiming that Oregon's law violates his or her constitutional right to equal protection because it discriminates between people who have the ability to take a lethal dose of pills and people who do not. The lawsuit would allege that in effect Oregon's law discriminates on the basis of physical disability. If a court were to accept this argument, then the court might hold that the person has the right to have a physician help him or her take the lethal dose of medication allowed under Oregon's law. This action amounts to voluntary euthanasia, and the hypothetical court case gives an example of how legalizing physician-assisted suicide could lead to the legalization of euthanasia.

Medical professor Robert Walker fears that legalized physician-assisted suicide could also prove to be a slippery slope toward involuntary euthanasia—in which a doctor ends a patient's life without the patient's consent. Under Oregon law, a person is ineligible for physician-assisted suicide if he or she is determined to be psychologically incapable of making an informed decision. Dr. Walker proposes a hypothetical lawsuit in which family members sue on behalf of a person who is determined not to be capable of making an informed decision:

> The plaintiff would have to argue that the incompetent patient has the same right to receive physician-assisted dying as those who retain their decisional capacity.

In other words, the family (or legal guardian) of a patient who was too depressed to make a rational decision would sue to enforce the patient's wishes. (Family members often make medical decisions for incapacitated patients based on either what the patient has said in the past or what they believe is in the patient's best interests.) The result, Dr. Walker fears, is that "[i]f the court accepts this framing of the issues, then it will likely remedy the inequity in the law by extending physician-assisted dying to incompetent, terminally ill patients."[8] After such a ruling, he argues, the physician and the family members would arrange for the physician to euthanize the patient without obtaining his or her express, informed consent—confirming the worst fears of people who believe that human life must be protected.

• **Are lawsuits like those described likely in states that legalize physician-assisted suicide?**

Opponents of physician-assisted suicide believe that there are valid, nonreligious reasons for prohibiting the practice, particularly fears based on abuses of euthanasia in Europe. They reject arguments that medical care prolongs life too long and becomes too expensive. They fear that legalizing physician-assisted suicide will lead down a "slippery slope" to involuntary euthanasia.

The Future of Physician-Assisted Suicide

F ive years after the Supreme Court ruled in *Glucksberg* and *Quill* that states could make their own laws regarding physician-assisted suicide, either prohibiting or allowing the practice, only Oregon has chosen to make the practice legal. In the meantime, advocates in other states have fought unsuccessfully for legalization. What does the future hold for physician-assisted suicide in the United States?

Supreme Court Trends

Although the Supreme Court ruled in *Glucksberg* and *Quill* that it would essentially leave decisions about physician-assisted suicide to the states, there is the possibility that the Court could revisit the issue. Each time a state passed a law, people in that state could challenge the law on any of a variety of grounds; perhaps one of those grounds would lead to a change in the

The future of assisted suicide, like that of many other issues in law and public policy, will be determined by the Supreme Court, whose composition changes as justices retire and are replaced. It is the Supreme Court that decides whether states have the power to prosecute those who assist suicides, and the Court's stand evolves with its composition. With the departure of Justice John Paul Stevens (seated, second from left), the Court may begin a conservative period and strengthen the states' banning power. Standing, from left, are Justices Ruth Bader Ginsburg, David Souter, Clarence Thomas, and Stephen Breyer; seated are Justices Antonin Scalia and John Paul Stevens, Chief Justice William H. Rehnquist, and Justices Sandra Day O'Connor and Anthony Kennedy.

Court's opinion. For example, disability groups might challenge a law allowing physician-assisted suicide on the grounds that it unfairly targets people with disabilities, or has a dispropor-tionate impact on people with disabilities.

In recent years, the Court has grown more conservative on many issues, especially abortion. Many advocates of civil liberties fear that the retirement of Justice John Paul Stevens, who was born in 1920, will lead the Court to shift even further to the right. Justice Stevens has been an ardent supporter of individual liberties. He wrote separately in *Glucksberg* that "some individuals who no longer have the option of deciding whether to live or to die because they are already on the threshold of death have a constitutionally protected interest that may outweigh the State's interest in preserving life at all costs." [1]

Civil libertarians fear that Stevens's eventual replacement will take a much narrower view of constitutional liberties, most likely agreeing with Chief Justice Rehnquist's view that the Constitution protects only acts that are "deeply rooted in this Nation's history and tradition." [2] If the Court does become more conservative, the possibility exists that states will have less latitude in legalizing physician-assisted suicide.

> • Is it right that the nine people on the Supreme Court have so much power in determining the meaning of the Constitution? How flexible is the Court?

Federal Law Enforcement

During the dual Clinton administration of 1992–2000, there was little federal interference with states' ability to legalize physician-assisted suicide. Although the Assisted Suicide Funding Restriction Act of 1997 prohibited the use of federal funds to pay for assisted suicide, the law did not in any way restrict the ability of doctors to legally (or illegally, for that matter) prescribe drugs for the purpose of assisting suicide.

When President George W. Bush took office and appointed John Ashcroft as attorney general, civil libertarians feared that the nation's top prosecutor would seek to curtail civil liberties in a number of areas, including abortion, free speech, disability rights, and privacy. In 2001, Ashcroft directed the federal Drug Enforcement Agency to enforce the Controlled Substances

Act (CSA) against Oregon doctors who prescribed controlled substances to patients for the purpose of assisting suicide.

A federal district judge blocked enforcement of Ashcroft's regulations, though, and it is unclear how the Supreme Court would resolve this apparent conflict between state and federal law. On the one hand, the conservative Supreme Court has tended to favor states' rights in recent years, but on the other hand, the Court's decisions have tended to restrict civil liberties. If Ashcroft appeals the decision all the way to the Supreme Court, then there may come a significant change in the way the law treats physician-assisted suicide.

- **Are state and federal laws equally important? If not, then which are more important?**

The Role of Public Opinion

Although a majority of Americans support physician-assisted suicide, supporters of legalization have yet to make a major impact in the state legislatures outside of Oregon. Why is this? There are several reasons why majority support for an idea does not necessarily translate into a law reflecting the majority opinion.

Often, people support a position when asked, but they do not care about the issue enough to work toward passage of a law supporting the position. For example, a majority of Americans may think that it would be nice to build a memorial in Washington, D.C., to honor the pioneers of American medicine— but very few of those people would want to see their taxes increased to make this happen, and fewer still would be willing to mount a march on Washington for the cause.

Passing a state law legalizing physician-assisted suicide would be difficult work, regardless of majority support. Backers of the law would likely face organized opposition from medical boards, churches, right-to-life organizations, and disability groups. The people who, in an opinion poll, expressed support for the law would not necessarily be willing to do the work necessary to convince legislators to pass a law. Even in states where a "ballot measure" allows the voters to vote directly on whether a proposition could become law, opponents of physician-assisted suicide are most likely better organized to influence public opinion and encourage people to vote than are supporters.

Perhaps people who support the basic concept of a physician assisting a dying patient in hastening death do not want to see the law officially condone such actions, preferring instead to allow it to continue unofficially. Many people probably do not

THE LETTER OF THE LAW

The Assisted Suicide Funding Restriction Act of 1997

(a) Findings. Congress finds the following:
   (1) The Federal Government provides financial support for the provision of and payment for health care services, as well as for advocacy activities to protect the rights of individuals.
   (2) Assisted suicide, euthanasia, and mercy killing have been criminal offenses throughout the United States and, under current law, it would be unlawful to provide services in support of such illegal activities.
   (3) Because of recent legal developments, it may become lawful in areas of the United States to furnish services in support of such activities.
   (4) Congress is not providing Federal financial assistance in support of assisted suicide, euthanasia, and mercy killing and intends that Federal funds not be used to promote such activities.
(b) Purpose. It is the principal purpose of this chapter to continue current Federal policy by providing explicitly that Federal funds may not be used to pay for items and services (including assistance) the purpose of which is to cause (or assist in causing) the suicide, euthanasia, or mercy killing of any individual.

Source: 42 U.S.C. §14401 (2000)

realize that it is exactly this type of unofficial recognition of euthanasia that led to serious abuses in the Netherlands.

Although public opinion has not yet led to widespread legalization of physician-assisted suicide, public opinion changes over time. Statistics indicate that younger people tend to favor physician-assisted suicide more than older people do. As the "baby boomers"—people born during a rapid growth in the U.S. population from the mid-1940s through the mid-1960s— begin to reach the age at which many of them will face serious illness, it is likely that public opinion will grow much stronger in favor of physician-assisted suicide. Whether this public opinion is strong enough to overcome the deeply entrenched opposition remains to be seen.

- **What other legal changes are likely as more and more "baby boomers" reach old age?**

Since 1997, the question of whether to legalize physician-assisted suicide has rested with state legislatures, but despite popular support, only Oregon has legalized the practice. At the federal level, the actions of the Supreme Court and the attorney general could also have an impact on the legalization and practice of physician-assisted suicide.

Death by Prescription

1 *Washington* v. *Glucksberg*, 521 U.S. 702 (1997).
2 *Vacco* v. *Quill*, 521 U.S. 793 (1997).
3 *Michigan* v. *Kevorkian*, No. 221758 (Mich. Ct. App. Nov. 20, 2001).
4 "New Poll Underscores National Support for Oregon's Law," Oregon Death with Dignity, press release, January 9, 2002 (citing data from Dec. 2001 Harris Interactive poll).
5 Wayne Guglielmo, "Assisted suicide? Pain control? Where's the line?" *Medical Economics* 19:48(2002).

Point: People Should Have the Right to Determine When and How They Die

1 *Washington* v. *Glucksberg*, 521 U.S. 702 (1997).
2 *Roe* v. *Wade*, 410 U.S. 113 (1973).
3 *Planned Parenthood of Southeastern Pennsylvania* v. *Casey*, 505 U.S. 833, 852 (1992).
4 Brief for Compassion in Dying, *Vacco* v. *Quill*, 521 U.S. 793 (1997) (No. 95–1858).
5 Ibid.
6 Barbara Coombs Lee, Testimony Before the U.S. House Subcommittee on the Constitution Concerning the Legality of Assisted Suicide, April 29, 1996, available online at *gos.sbc.edu/l/lee.html*.
7 Stand. Com. Rep. No.539–02 Re: H.B. No. 2487 (A Bill for an Act Relating to Death with Dignity) (report of Committee on Judiciary and Hawaiian Affairs), 2002 Legislative Session, available online at *www.capitol.hawaii.gov/sessioncurrent/ commreports/hb2487_hd1_hscr539-02_.htm*.
8 Legislative guidelines available online at *www.hemlock.org*.
9 *Quill* v. *Vacco*, 80 F.3d 716 (2d Cir. 1996).
10 Ibid.
11 Barbara Coombs Lee, Testimony Before the U.S. House Subcommittee on the Constitution Concerning the Legality of Assisted Suicide, April 29, 1996, available online at *gos.sbc.edu/l/lee.html*.
12 Brief for Coalition of Hospice and Palliative Care Professionals, *Washington* v. *Glucksberg*, 521 U.S. 702 (1997) (No. 96–110) and *Vacco* v. *Quill*, 521 U.S. 793 (1997) (No. 95–1858).

Counterpoint: States Should Protect People from Choosing Suicide

1 United States Catholic Conference, *Catechism of the Catholic Church*, 2d ed. §§ 2259–2283 (1994).
2 Brief for Bioethics Professors, *Washington* v. *Glucksberg*, 521 U.S. 702 (1997) (No. 96–110) and *Vacco* v. *Quill*, 521 U.S. 793 (1997) (No. 95–1858).
3 *Washington* v. *Glucksberg*, 521 U.S. 702 (1997).
4 *Cruzan* v. *Director, Mo. Dept. of Health*, 497 U.S. 261 (1990).
5 Ibid.
6 Ezekiel Emanuel, "Whose Right to Die?" *The Atlantic Monthly*, 279 Vol. 3 (March 1997), pp. 73–79.
7 *Washington* v. *Glucksberg*, 521 U.S. 702 (1997).
8 *Cruzan* v. *Director, Mo. Dept. of Health*, 497 U.S. 261 (1990).
9 *Washington* v. *Glucksberg*, 521 U.S. 702 (1997) (Souter, J., concurring in the judgments).
10 Linda Ganzini, et al., "Physicians' Experiences with the Oregon Death with Dignity Act," *New England Journal of Medicine*, 342:8 (February 24, 2000):557.
11 National Right to Life Committee, profile of Robert Provan, available online at *www.euthanasia.com/case1.html*.

Point: People Should Not Have to Make End-of-Life Decisions Without Medical Advice

1 Brief for American Medical Students Association, *Washington* v. *Glucksberg*, 521 U.S. 702 (1997) (No. 96–110) and *Vacco* v. *Quill*, 521 U.S. 793 (1997) (No. 95–1858).
2 Timothy E. Quill, Barbara Coombs Lee, and Sally J. Nunn, "Palliative Treatments of Last Resort," in *Assisted Suicide: Finding Common Ground*, eds. Lois Snyder and Arthur L. Caplan, Indiana University Press, 2002, p. 71.
3 Brief for Law Professors, *Washington* v. *Glucksberg*, 521 U.S. 702 (1997) (No. 96–110) and *Vacco* v. *Quill*, 521 U.S. 793 (1997) (No. 95–1858), quoting Timothy Quill, "Death and Dignity: A Case of Individualized Decision Making," *New England Journal of Medicine*, 324(1991):691, 693.

4 Brief for Law Professors, *Washington* v. *Glucksberg*, 521 U.S. 702 (1997) (No. 96–110) and *Vacco* v. *Quill*, 521 U.S. 793 (1997) (No. 95–1858), quoting Timothy Quill, "Death and Dignity: A Case of Individualized Decision Making," *New England Journal of Medicine*, 324(1991):691, 693.

5 Derek Humphrey, *Final Exit: The Practicalities of Self-Deliverance and Assisted Suicide for the Dying*, 2d ed., DTP, 1997.

6 Brief for Law Professors, *Washington* v. *Glucksberg*, 521 U.S. 702 (1997) (No. 96–110) and *Vacco* v. *Quill*, 521 U.S. 793 (1997) (No. 95–1858).

7 Interview with Arthur Caplan, aired on *Frontline*, May 14, 1996. Transcript available online at *www.pbs.org/wgbh/pages/frontline/kevorkian/medicine/caplan1.html*.

Counterpoint: Widespread Legalization Would Have Devastating Effects on Medical Practice and Research

1 Wayne Guglielmo, "Assisted Suicide? Pain Control? Where's the Line?" *Medical Economics*, 19(2002):48.

2 See MedHelpNet.com, "The Oath and Law of Hippocrates," available online at *www.medhelpnet.com/oath.html*.

3 American Medical Association, Ethics Opinion §2.211, "Physician-Assisted Suicide," 1996.

4 Bernard Baumrin, "Physician, Stay Thy Hand!" in *Physician Assisted Suicide: Expanding the Debate*, eds. Margaret P. Battin, Rosamond Rhodes, and Anita Silvers, Routledge, 1998, p. 179.

5 *Oregon* v. *Ashcroft*, No. 01-1647-JO (D. Ore. April 17, 2002).

6 Ezekiel Emanuel, "Whose Right to Die?" *The Atlantic Monthly*, 279:3(March 1997):73.

7 Budget Hearings Before the Subcommittees on Labor, Health and Human Services, Education, and Related Agencies of the House Committee on Appropriations. (Statement of American Liver Foundation, March 14, 2001).

8 ALS Association, "Promising Areas in ALS Research," available online at *www.alsa.org/challenge/promise.cfm*.

9 Ryan White Comprehensive AIDS Resources Emergency (CARE) Act, Public Law No. 101–381 (Aug. 18, 1990).

10 "Addressing Racial and Ethnic Disparities in Health Care" (publication no. 00-PO41), fact sheet, Agency for Healthcare Research and Quality, February 2000, available online at *www.ahrq.gov/research/disparit.htm*.

11 "Frail, Elderly Patients More Opposed to Physician-Assisted Suicide than Younger Relatives," press release, Duke University Medical Center, October 22, 1996.

12 Focus on the Family, "Physician-Assisted Suicide and Euthanasia," March 1, 2001, available online at *www.family.org/cforum/research/papers/a0015056.html*.

Point: Modern Medicine Has Increased the Need for Physician-Assisted Suicide

1 Statistics supplied by Centers for Disease Control and Prevention, available online at *www.cdc.gov/nchs/fastats/lifexpec.htm*.

2 Jack Kevorkian, *Prescription: Medicine*, Prometheus Books, 1991, p. 186. The term *dis-ease* appears in the original text.

3 Federal Interagency Forum on Aging-Related Statistics, *Older Americans 2000: Key Indicators of Well-Being*. U.S. Government Printing Office, August 2000.

4 Jack Kevorkian, *Prescription: Medicine*, Prometheus Books, 1991, p. 186.

5 "Fewer Oregonians Used Death with Dignity Act in 2001," press release, Oregon Public Health Services, February 6, 2002.

6 Brief for Compassion in Dying, *Vacco* v. *Quill*, 521 U.S. 793 (1997) (No. 95–1858).

7 "New Poll Underscores National Support for Oregon's Law," press release, Oregon Death with Dignity, January 9, 2002 (citing data from December 2001 Harris Interactive poll).

8 Jack Kevorkian, *Prescription: Medicine*, Prometheus Books, 1991, p. 240.

9 Raphael Cohen-Almagor, *The Right to Die with Dignity: An Argument in Ethics, Medicine, and Law*, Rutgers University Press, 2001, p. 3.

10 Arthur L. Caplan, Lois Snyder, and Kathy Faber-Langendoen, "The Role of Guidelines in the Practice of Physician-Assisted Suicide," in *Assisted Suicide: Finding Common Ground*, eds. Lois Snyder and Arthur L. Caplan, Indiana University Press, 2002, p. 40.

11 See *www.dwd.org/fss/impactanalysis.asp.*
12 Brief for Coalition of Hospice and Palliative Care Professionals, *Washington v. Glucksberg*, 521 U.S. 702 (1997) (No. 96–110) and *Vacco v. Quill*, 521 U.S. 793 (1997) (No. 95–1858).
13 Brief for Compassion in Dying, *Vacco v. Quill*, 521 U.S. 793 (1997) (No. 95–1858).
14 Wayne Guglielmo, "Assisted Suicide? Pain Control? Where's the Line?" *Medical Economics*, 19(2002):48.
15 *Cruzan v. Director, Mo. Dept. of Health*, 497 U.S. 261 (1990).
16 American Medical Association, Policy H-140.966, "Decisions Near the End of Life."
17 Wayne Guglielmo, "Assisted Suicide? Pain Control? Where's the Line?" *Medical Economics*, 19(2002):48.
18 American Medical Association, Policy H-140.966, "Decisions Near the End of Life."

2 "Disability Advocates Relieved over Defeat of Assisted Suicide," press release, Not Dead Yet, 2002, available online at *www.notdeadyet.org/docs/press11.html.*
3 Margaret Somerville, *Death Talk: The Case Against Euthanasia and Physician-Assisted Suicide*, McGill-Queens University Press, 2001, p. 50.
4 *Washington v. Glucksberg*, 521 U.S. 702 (1997).
5 John D. Arras, "Physician-Assisted Suicide: A Tragic View," in *Physician Assisted Suicide: Expanding the Debate*, ed. Margaret P. Battin, Rosamond Rhodes, and Anita Silvers, Routledge, 1998, p. 285.
6 Brief for Compassion in Dying, *Washington v. Glucksberg*, 521 U.S. 702 (1997) (No. 96–110).
7 *Vacco v. Quill*, 521 U.S. 793 (1997).
8 Robert M. Walker: "Physician-Assisted Suicide: The Legal Slippery Slope," *Cancer Control*, 8:1(January/February 2001).

Counterpoint: Nothing Justifies Taking a Human Life

1 Gabrielle Degroot Redford, "Their Final Answers," *Modern Maturity* (September/October 2000), available online at *www.aarp.org/mmaturity/sept_oct00/finalanswers.html.*

The Future of Physician-Assisted Suicide

1 *Washington v. Glucksberg*, 521 U.S. 702 (1997) (Stevens, J., concurring in the judgments).
2 *Washington v. Glucksberg*, 521 U.S. 702 (1997).

General Resources on Physician-Assisted Suicide

Battin, Margaret P., Rosamond Rhodes, and Anita Silvers, eds. *Physician Assisted Suicide: Expanding the Debate.* Routledge, 1998.

Beauchamp, Tom L., and Seymour Perlin, eds. *Ethical Issues in Death and Dying.* Prentice-Hall, 1978.

Betzold, Michael. *Appointment with Doctor Death.* Momentum Books, 1993.

Prado, C.G., ed. *Assisted Suicide: Canadian Perspectives.* University of Ottawa Press, 2000.

Snyder, Lois, and Arthur L. Caplan, eds. *Assisted Suicide: Finding Common Grounds.* Indiana University Press, 2002.

Longwood University: Doctor Assisted Suicide: A Guide to Web Sites and the Literature
www.longwood.edu/library/suic.htm
Longwood University's library features a substantial section on its website about researching physician-assisted suicide, including a bibliography.

University of Pennsylvania: Center for Bioethics: Physician-Assisted Suicide: Amicus Briefs
www.med.upenn.edu/bioethic/PAS/
Arthur Caplan of the University of Pennsylvania's Center for Bioethics is a nationally recognized expert on the subject of physician-assisted suicide. The website contains links to many vital legal documents.

For Legalization

Cohen-Almagor, Raphael. *The Right to Die with Dignity: An Argument in Ethics, Medicine, and Law.* Rutgers University Press, 2001.

Kevorkian, Jack. *Prescription: Medicine.* Buffalo: Prometheus Books, 1991.

The Compassion in Dying Federation
www.compassionindying.org
The national organization that unsuccessfully challenged Washington's ban on physician-assisted suicide in *Washington* v. *Glucksberg.* Advocates nationally for laws legalizing the practice.

The Hemlock Society
www.hemlock.org
National organization that educates members about suicide options and advocates for legalization of physician-assisted suicide.

Oregon Death with Dignity

www.dwd.org
Oregon-based group that successfully fought for passage of the Oregon Death With Dignity Act, the first law in the United States to legalize physician-assisted suicide explicitly. Offers assistance to groups in other states.

Against Legalization

Gill, Robin, ed. *Euthanasia and the Churches.* Cassell, 2000.

Somerville, Margaret. *Death Talk: The Case Against Euthanasia and Physician-Assisted Suicide.* McGill-Queens University Press, 2001.

The International Task Force on Euthanasia and Assisted Suicide

www.euthanasia.com
International organization opposing legalization of euthanasia and physician-assisted suicide.

Focus on the Family

www.family.org
National organization dedicated to conservative, "pro-family" causes; opposes physician-assisted suicide largely on moral grounds.

Not Dead Yet

www.notdeadyet.org
Organization of people with disabilities; strongly opposes physician-assisted suicide as "legalized killing" and a form of discrimination.

Oregon Right to Life: Assisted Suicide

www.ortl.org/suicide.htm
Group favoring repeal of Oregon's law allowing physician-assisted suicide. This website focuses on the Oregon situation but offers many documents of interest to the researcher of larger constitutional issues.

***Cruzan* v. *Director, Mo. Dept. of Health*,** 497 U.S. 261 (1990)
Held that a person has a constitutional right to refuse unwanted medical treatment, but that a state also has a strong interest in protecting the lives of its citizens and can therefore require "clear and convincing evidence" that a person wants to refuse treatment.

The Natural Death Act of 1992, Wash. Rev. Code §§ 70.122.010–70.122.100 (2002)
Washington state law allowing the termination of life support but not physician-assisted suicide.

***Washington* v. *Glucksberg*,** 521 U.S. 702 (1997)
Held that Washington's Natural Death Act, which prohibited physician-assisted suicide, did not violate the due process clause of the U.S. Constitution because a decision to commit suicide is not a "fundamental liberty."

***Vacco* v. *Quill*,** 521 U.S. 793 (1997)
Held that New York did not violate the equal protection clause of the U.S. Constitution by allowing some people to refuse life support while preventing others from committing suicide with the assistance of a physician; the two acts are significantly different and the state has rational reasons to prohibit assisting suicide.

The Assisted Suicide Funding Restriction Act of 1997, 42 U.S.C. § 14401 (2000)
Federal law prohibiting the use of federal funds for assisted suicide.

The Death with Dignity Act of 1997, Or. Rev. Stat. §§ 127.800–127.897 (2001)
Oregon state law legalizing physician-assisted suicide for terminally ill people, subject to certain safeguards.

***Michigan* v. *Kevorkian*,** No. 221758 (Mich. Ct. App. Nov. 20, 2001)
Upheld Jack Kevorkian's conviction for second-degree murder in the case of Thomas Youk, whom Kevorkian injected with lethal doses of medication.

***Oregon* v. *Ashcroft*,** No. 01-1647-JO (D. Ore. April 17, 2002)
Federal trial judge rules that U.S. attorney general cannot prosecute Oregon physicians for prescribing lethal medications in compliance with the state's Death With Dignity Act.

Concepts and Standards

physician-assisted suicide
euthanasia (voluntary/involuntary)
life support
terminal sedation
living will
palliative care
Hippocratic Oath
managed care

"right to die"
"right to life"
"death with dignity"
competence
"slippery slope" arguments
due process clause
equal protection clause

Beginning Legal Research

The goal of POINT/COUNTERPOINT is not only to provide the reader with an introduction to a controversial issue affecting society, but also to encourage the reader to explore the issue more fully. This appendix, then, is meant to serve as a guide to the reader in researching the current state of the law as well as exploring some of the public-policy arguments as to why existing laws should be changed or new laws are needed.

Like many types of research, legal research has become much faster and more accessible with the invention of the Internet. This appendix discusses some of the best starting points, but of course "surfing the Net" will uncover endless additional sources of information—some more reliable than others. Some important sources of law are not yet available on the Internet, but these can generally be found at the larger public and university libraries. Librarians usually are happy to point patrons in the right direction.

The most important source of law in the United States is the Constitution. Originally enacted in 1787, the Constitution outlines the structure of our federal government and sets limits on the types of laws that the federal government and state governments can pass. Through the centuries, a number of amendments have been added to or changed in the Constitution, most notably the first ten amendments, known collectively as the Bill of Rights, which guarantee important civil liberties. Each state also has its own constitution, many of which are similar to the U.S. Constitution. It is important to be familiar with the U.S. Constitution because so many of our laws are affected by its requirements. State constitutions often provide protections of individual rights that are even stronger than those set forth in the U.S. Constitution.

Within the guidelines of the U.S. Constitution, Congress—both the House of Representatives and the Senate—passes bills that are either vetoed or signed into law by the President. After the passage of the law, it becomes part of the United States Code, which is the official compilation of federal laws. The state legislatures use a similar process, in which bills become law when signed by the state's governor. Each state has its own official set of laws, some of which are published by the state and some of which are published by commercial publishers. The U.S. Code and the state codes are an important source of legal research; generally, legislators make efforts to make the language of the law as clear as possible.

However, reading the text of a federal or state law generally provides only part of the picture. In the American system of government, after the legislature passes laws and the executive (U.S. President or state governor) signs them, it is up to the judicial branch of the government, the court system, to interpret the laws and decide whether they violate any provision of the Constitution. At the state level, each state's supreme court has the ultimate authority in determining what a law means and whether or not it violates the state constitution. However, the federal courts—headed by the U.S. Supreme Court—can review state laws and court decisions to determine whether they violate federal laws or the U.S. Constitution. For example, a state court may find that a particular criminal law is valid under the state's constitution, but a federal court may then review the state court's decision and determine that the law is invalid under the U.S. Constitution.

It is important, then, to read court decisions when doing legal research. The Constitution uses language that is intentionally very general—for example, prohibiting "unreasonable searches and seizures" by the police—and court cases often provide more guidance. For example, the U.S. Supreme Court's 2001 decision in *Kyllo* v. *United States* held that scanning the outside of a person's house using a heat sensor to determine whether the person is growing marijuana is unreasonable—*if* it is done without a search warrant secured from a judge. Supreme Court decisions provide the most definitive explanation of the law of the land, and it is therefore important to include these in research. Often, when the Supreme Court has not decided a case on a particular issue, a decision by a federal appeals court or a state supreme court can provide guidance; but just as laws and constitutions can vary from state to state, so can federal courts be split on a particular interpretation of federal law or the U.S. Constitution. For example, federal appeals courts in Louisiana and California may reach opposite conclusions in similar cases.

Lawyers and courts refer to statutes and court decisions through a formal system of citations. Use of these citations reveals which court made the decision (or which legislature passed the statute) and when and enables the reader to locate the statute or court case quickly in a law library. For example, the legendary Supreme Court case *Brown* v. *Board of Education* has the legal citation 347 U.S. 483 (1954). At a law library, this 1954 decision can be found on page 483 of volume 347 of the U.S. Reports, the official collection of the Supreme Court's decisions. Citations can also be helpful in locating court cases on the Internet.

Understanding the current state of the law leads only to a partial understanding of the issues covered by the POINT/COUNTERPOINT series. For a fuller understanding of the issues, it is necessary to look at public-policy arguments that the current state of the law is not adequately addressing the issue. Many groups lobby for new legislation or changes to existing legislation; the National Rifle Association (NRA), for example, lobbies Congress and the state legislatures constantly to make existing gun control laws less restrictive and not to pass additional laws. The NRA and other groups dedicated to various causes might also intervene in pending court cases: a group such as Planned Parenthood might file a brief *amicus curiae* (as "a friend of the court")—called an "amicus brief"—in a lawsuit that could affect abortion rights. Interest groups also use the media to influence public opinion, issuing press releases and frequently appearing in interviews on news programs and talk shows. The books in POINT/COUNTERPOINT list some of the interest groups that are active in the issue at hand, but in each case there are countless other groups working at the local, state, and national levels. It is important to read everything with a critical eye, for sometimes interest groups present information in a way that can be read only to their advantage. The informed reader must always look for bias.

Finding sources of legal information on the Internet is relatively simple thanks to "portal" sites such as FindLaw (*www.findlaw.com*), which provides access to a variety of constitutions, statutes, court opinions, law review articles, news articles, and other resources—including all Supreme Court decisions issued since 1893. Other useful sources of information include the U.S. Government Printing Office (*www.gpo.gov*), which contains a complete copy of the U.S. Code, and the Library of Congress's THOMAS system (*thomas.loc.gov*), which offers access to bills pending before Congress as well as recently passed laws. Of course, the Internet changes every second of every day, so it is best to do some independent searching. Most cases, studies, and opinions that are cited or referred to in public debate can be found online—and *everything* can be found in one library or another.

The Internet can provide a basic understanding of most important legal issues, but not all sources can be found there. To find some documents it is necessary to visit the law library of a university or a public law library; some cities have public law libraries, and many library systems keep legal documents at the main branch. On the following page are some common citation forms.

COMMON CITATION FORMS

Source of Law	Sample Citation	Notes
U.S. Supreme Court	*Employment Division v. Smith*, 485 U.S. 660 (1988)	The U.S. Reports is the official record of Supreme Court decisions. There is also an unofficial Supreme Court ("S.Ct.") reporter.
U.S. Court of Appeals	*United States v. Lambert*, 695 F.2d 536 (11th Cir. 1983)	Appellate cases appear in the Federal Reporter, designated by "F." The 11th Circuit has jurisdiction in Alabama, Florida, and Georgia.
U.S. District Court	*Carillon Importers, Ltd. v. Frank Pesce Group, Inc.*, 913 F.Supp. 1559 (S.D.Fla.1996)	Federal trial-level decisions are reported in the Federal Supplement ("F.Supp."). Some states have multiple federal districts; this case originated in the Southern District of Florida.
U.S. Code	Thomas Jefferson Commemoration Commission Act, 36 U.S.C., §149 (2002)	Sometimes the popular names of legislation—names with which the public may be familiar—are included with the U.S. Code citation.
State Supreme Court	*Sterling v. Cupp*, 290 Ore. 611, 614, 625 P.2d 123, 126 (1981)	The Oregon Supreme Court decision is reported in both the state's reporter and the Pacific regional reporter.
State statute	Pennsylvania Abortion Control Act of 1982, 18 Pa. Cons. Stat. 3203-3220 (1990)	States use many different citation formats for their statutes.

109

110

111

ALAN MARZILLI, of Durham, North Carolina, is an independent consultant working on several ongoing projects for state and federal government agencies and nonprofit organizations. He has spoken about mental health issues in more than 20 states, the District of Columbia, and Puerto Rico; his work includes training mental health administrators, nonprofit management and staff, and people with mental illness and their family members on a wide variety of topics, including effective advocacy, community-based mental health services, and housing. He has written several handbooks and training curricula that are used nationally. He managed statewide and national mental health advocacy programs and worked for several public interest lobbying organizations in Washington, D.C., while studying law at Georgetown University.